REF
LB
2840
.T47

Thomas, Andrew C.

Major issues in
educational
psychology as
applied to the
classroom teacher

DATE

REFERENCE

Cop.1

FORM 125 M

SOCIAL SCIENCES AND HISTORY DIVISION

The Chicago Public Library

APR 4 - 1979

Received

© THE BAKER & TAYLOR CO.

MAJOR ISSUES IN EDUCATIONAL PSYCHOLOGY AS APPLIED TO THE CLASSROOM TEACHER

Andrew C. Thomas
Ben E. Pitts
Jettie M. McWilliams
Tennessee Technological University
Cookeville, Tennessee

KENDALL/HUNT PUBLISHING COMPANY
2460 Kerper Boulevard, Dubuque, Iowa 52001

Copyright © 1977 by Andrew C. Thomas, Ben E. Pitts, and Jettie M. McWilliams

Library of Congress Catalog Card Number: 77—84530

ISBN 0—8403—1802—2

All rights reserved. No part of this publication may be reproduced, stored in a retrieval system, or transmitted, in any form or by any means, electronic, mechanical, photocopying, recording, or otherwise, without the prior written permission of the copyright owner.

Printed in the United States of America

401802   01

PREFACE

There is a growing desire among state educational agencies to have teachers become interested in and discriminating consumers of educational research. *Major Issues in Educational Psychology as Applied to the Classroom Teacher* meets that need. This textbook begins with the library and integrates library usage throughout the text. It is based on the philosophical statement that an effective teacher must possess informational skills to meet the onslaught of a rapidly changing scientific and technological world.

No longer can students rely on textbook information because it can often be outdated and out of tune with current practices. This textbook refers to current research and encourages students to gather information concerning major issues in educational psychology. Once this information is collected, it is then synthesized in groups within the classroom. It is the belief of the authors that the practice of seeking out current information and applying it to the classroom will carry over into the professional life of the students once they have graduated into a highly competitive job market.

Background information is provided by the textbook on the major issues in educational psychology. This background places the issue in historical perspective, identifies various points of view, and cites current research trends in the area. Eight major issues in educational psychology are focused on. These are informational skills, constructing behavioral objectives, discipline, motivation, learning, personality, and student evaluation. These chapters are written in a straightforward manner in a language college students can understand. Behavioral objectives were constructed and placed at the end of each chapter. The purpose was to aid the student in studying and sorting out the major concepts.

The issues are limited so the student can gain a clear perspective of the field of educational psychology. This simple clear approach fosters exploration of current literature available in the field.

Acknowledgments

This book was shaped by the instructors in their day-to-day classroom activities. Dr. Homer Kemp polished and edited the manuscript into its final form. The authors also wish to express appreciation to Mrs. Homer Kemp for her invaluable typing services.

The authors express appreciation to Mr. Milton Minor, media specialist at Tennessee Technological University, for his illustration and photographs.

Deep appreciation is expressed to Sheila Hix, Velda Koger, and Sharon Marlow for their help securing photographs and material for the book.

CONTENTS

Chapter 1: The Library, **1**
    The Problem, **3**
    Finding Information, **10**
    Organizing the Information Center, **14**
    Notes on Notetaking Center, **16**
    Education Resources Information Centers, **16**
    Summary, **19**

Chapter 2: Personality Theories, **21**
    Psychoanalytic Theory, **21**
    Using Psychoanalytic Concepts in the Classroom, **25**
    Humanistic Theories of Personality, **26**
    Using Humanistic Psychology in the Classroom, **28**
    Learning Theories, **28**
    Summary, **28**
    Student Objectives, **29**

Chapter 3: The Development of Personality, **31**
    Heredity, **31**
    Cultural Influence on Development, **33**
    Emotional Development, **36**
    Summary, **37**
    Student Objectives, **37**

Chapter 4: Motivation, **39**
    Psychological Concepts of Motivation, **40**
    Extrinsic Motivation, **55**
    Intrinsic Motivation, **56**
    Practical Classroom Applications of Psychological Concepts, **58**
    Summary, **59**
    Student Objectives, **60**

Chapter 5: Learning, **61**
    Types of Learning, **63**
    Positive Reinforcement, Negative Reinforcement, Punishment, and Their Consequences, **67**
    Retention, **72**

Transfer, **74**
Summary, **76**
Student Objectives, **76**

Chapter 6: Discipline, **79**

Types of Conduct Problems, **81**
Solutions to Misbehavior Problems, **92**
Current Research, **99**
Summary, **100**
Student Objectives, **101**

Chapter 7: Student Evaluation, **103**

Intelligence, **103**
Theories of Intelligence, **104**
Summary, **119**
Student Objectives, **119**

Chapter 8: Behavioral Objectives, **121**

Historical Perspective, **121**
Definitions, **124**
Bloom's Taxonomy, **125**
Considerations, **128**
Construction, **128**
Advantages, **130**
Summary, **131**
Student Objectives, **132**

References, **133**

Chapter 1
THE LIBRARY

The study of educational psychology includes looking at the relationship between teaching and learning. Many of the psychological principles to be discussed in this text have evolved from laboratory studies of individual and group learning processes. Educational psychology is not a static course to be studied by the student. It is viable, ever growing and changing. To enable the student and teacher to obtain accurate and current information, the acquisition and utilization of library skills is essential.

The search for information will be the major concern in this chapter, and, though the search may be time consuming, it is a necessary part of educational inquiry. The college or university library is a valuable source of information. Skill in the use of the library is necessary to efficiently and effectively locate information related to a specific problem under investigation.

After the student has formulated a problem clearly, he must learn whether the question has been answered by someone else and must frequently gather information from areas closely related to the problem. Most of what is known can be found in libraries in various forms. Every year thousands of books, monographs, journals, documents, and other materials are added to libraries. This body of knowledge is essential to the person who seeks answers to questions that arise, and can be used to provide a sound basis for further searching for answers through research studies.

Skillful use of the library gives direction to the specialized materials needed for a comprehensive search for all possible information related to a study. An attempt to find needed material without library skills results in much wasted effort. An evening wasted in the library can be one of the most frustrating experiences for a student; or an evening during which the time is used efficiently can be rewarding both in the material located and in achieving a personal accomplishment. This chapter is designed to help students make trips to the library personally rewarding and productive and to present guidelines for evaluating research found in libraries.

Practically all knowledge of man can be found in books and periodicals housed in library collections.

THE PROBLEM

Before research is undertaken two requirements are made of the student:

1. A definition of the problem.
2. How to evaluate the literature once it is found.

The following set of guidelines constitutes a type of instrument for analyzing research reports. It consists of twenty criteria which are self-explanatory, relatively obvious and simple to apply, and which deal with some features of research reporting that are sometimes overlooked. These guidelines may be useful to the ever-growing number of students taking courses in educational research, to neophyte practitioners in research, to consumers of educational research, and to those who must judge them.

In the analysis of a research report, the guidelines should be strictly followed in the order given. It is best to read the report several times and then write out the analysis step by step in a clear and straightforward manner. Opinions should be expressed with vigor about each facet of the report, for a critique is no place for polite subtlety. An analysis is not to be just a written summary or resume' of the report—although enough of the project should be explained so that it can be fully understood—nor is it to be a term paper, but a critique; therefore, it must be critical. On the other hand, credit should be given where credit is deserved, and the report should be praised for its good points, while it is criticized for what is bad. If some aspects of the report are not understood, this fact should be admitted by the critic for his own intellectual honesty and integrity. It should also be noted that the editor of the publication sometimes makes changes, particularly to save space. The overall aim should be to express a healthy skepticism without falling victim to cynicism. Finally, the entire analysis should be rewritten at least twice.

1. Problem raised. A problem is a felt need or difficulty. It should be obviously important and worthwhile and should have a reasonable chance of being solved without excess time and effort. A problem properly posed and stated in declarative or question form is the base upon which the research project is built. Natural scientists say "that a problem well stated is a problem half solved." It must therefore be in terms which are succinct, specific, and precise so that it leads naturally to all the subsequent steps. An unspecified, vague, implied or poorly delineated problem is a serious handicap to the researcher, for an investigator who begins his study in confusion ends in confusion.

2. Previous work cited. There should be evidence of a good literature search and an adequate grasp of the current "state of the art." Failure to cite previous studies implies laziness or ignorance. The most recent papers deserve the most attention because they provide the most recent findings

and include older sources. While previous papers should be documented and critically appraised by the researcher, too much detail or a long list of references are not necessary and serve only to "clutter" the effort. A good project sets out to replicate or extend the previous work with improvements relative to reducing bias, eliminating flaws, considering pertinent variables, resolving issues, or checking contradictory or uncertain findings.

3. Objectives stated. These objectives are the ultimate goals, the social rationale for solving the problem. They should be limited to one, be important, and specific in scope so that they can be broken down into a group of clearly defined hypotheses.

4. Hypotheses formulated. A common error is to present several objectives and only one or two hypotheses. This should be the reverse. Hypotheses are reasonable and narrow generalizations which are to be tested during the study. They must be either accepted or rejected. Therefore, the mark of excellence of a good hypothesis is that it can be tested. Hypotheses may be stated as either positive or negative. Negative hypotheses are called "null hypotheses."

5. Assumptions made. It is impossible for an investigator to control all the components in his project; therefore, he must base his work on several assumptions, similar to axioms in geometric proofs. An assumption is a reasonable but presently unprovable factor. The more rigorous the research, the fewer the assumptions. Consequently, every assumption should be justified.

(Note: In some published papers, the authors may not state explicitly one or more of the above criteria, and it is important to the reader to form them from other portions of the report or by inference.)

6. Population stated. By definition, a population must be clearly described by its characteristics and size. The reasons for selecting the chosen population should be well explained. It cannot be assumed to be a normal population unless it is large and heterogeneous; otherwise the normal distribution must be proved.

7. Sample drawn. The sample is a key factor on which many projects fail. A true sample must be representative of the population, otherwise the sample must be drawn by using a table of random numbers so that every member of the population has an equal chance of being selected. In either case the procedure is difficult and complex and the size and nature of the sample must be defended as appropriate. A small sample selected by using a good technique is better than a large sample poorly selected. A control group must be chosen with equal care.

8. Instruments used. Poor instrumentation is another common and serious flaw which plagues educational research. To make certain that the

instruments will accurately and consistently measure what is to be measured, they should have been pretested in a pilot study. A "faint tinge of validity and reliability" is not adequate. Any original instrument should be fully illustrated and described. It is ridiculous for a researcher who has formed an untested measuring device to claim that the results he obtains with its use can be accepted with any degree of assurance.

9. Design examined. In general, the simpler the experimental design, the better. Elaborate designs may attempt too much, and cause the study to get bogged down. Treatments and data-collection methods should be clearly delineated. Variables should be recognized, identified as dependent or independent, and controls employed whenever possible. The statistical procedures should be a part of the design from the first, not applied after the data have been collected.

10. Procedure followed. A goal procedure is a hallmark of good reports. The steps in carrying out the project should be described in complete detail so they can be understood; the measure of success for procedure is that the entire process could be replicated by another investigator who would wish to do so.

11. Safeguards taken. Many sources of error and bias creep into research. Some of these may be anticipated and guarded against. Ample time is one safeguard which allows for Murphy's Law, which says that "If there is anything which can possibly go wrong in research, it usually does." Sampling adequately, pretesting instruments, training assistants, controlling some variables, eliminating the "hallo" effect, refining procedures, allowing for errors, and calling on experts for assistance are some other precautions.

12. Observations recorded. These are the raw, primary sources of data. Observations consist of such elements as test scores and other values measured by the instruments, replies to questionnaires, checklists, rating scales, oral or written reactions, lists of activities, and overt behavior.

13. Findings assembled. Observations are generally stated in summary form such as tables, graphs, and charts. Tabulations should be as simple as possible and all parts of tables, such as abbreviations, should be explained. Technical jargon should be minimized, for the best tables are those that are self-explanatory to the careful reader. If the reports do not include the tabulated findings, all conclusions and interpretations may be viewed with suspicion.

14. Statistics interpreted. A research report filled with statistical jargon should be regarded with a degree of skepticism. It may represent an attempt to impress the reader, to substitute technicalities for understanding, to counterfeit accuracy or to cover unpalatable facts. In educational research the interest lies in estimating how much the results could have been

the result of chance and how much could be ascribed to the treatments used in the procedure. The current practice is to allow no more than five percent to chance in order to have the results regarded as statistically significant. This is written as "at the .05 level of confidence of," if expressed as a probability that chance played a role and the greater the assurance that the treatments did so. The confidence level or P value is found in the proper tables after applying the t-test, the chi square technique or the analysis of variance—depending on the kinds of data and the utilization of them.

15. Interpretations discussed. Discussing interpretations refers to what the investigator's findings mean to him in terms of his study. Since some readers may look at the same data and derive other meanings, all tabulations must be included in the report. The author should also discuss the implications, usefulness and benefits of his findings. A common error of researchers is their failure to examine their own findings from different points of view and to extract all possible meanings from the data.

16. Conclusions reached. Essentially, this consists of the acceptance or the rejection of the hypotheses which have been proposed at the outset of the study. Some workers find it difficult to face the reality of negative conclusions and failures as thoroughly respectable and worthwhile reporting. Four common and serious flaws may crop up. One flaw is to rationalize away the breakdown of the stated hypotheses and to bring new elements not previously stated into the report. Another is to extrapolate the findings and conclusions to situations and to populations not represented in the subpopulations under investigation. A third is to lean on the "fudge factor" or "stretch factor" to reach the expected conclusions. A fourth, and most serious, is to draw conclusions not justified by the findings.

17. Limitations recognized. No matter how carefully planned and executed, every research effort has limitations and weaknesses which may or may not be the fault of the investigator. Regardless, it is his obligation to be intellectually honest and aware, pointing out limitations as a caution to research consumers and as a guide for future workers in the area.

18. Further work projected. Work on one problem generally gives rise to different problems. The problem may be the next logical step, some new related hypothesis, the application of different techniques, improved design, better instruments or a more representative sample.

19. Improvements suggested. Valuable ideas may be proposed by the reader as to how the project or the reporting of it could have been improved. A good understanding of the study, plus hindsight and a different

point of view, will produce suggestions as to how the study could have been better controlled and how pitfalls could have been avoided.

20. Clarity of report. The published paper should be written in plain, straightforward language and be easy to follow and understand. Jargon, verbiage, undefined terms, and meticulous descriptions indicate that the author did not understand what he was doing, cannot express himself meaningfully, or is trying to impress the reader. A poorly organized paper may be the result of haste, carelessness, or lack of understanding. If the research report cannot be easily understood by a serious reader—the prospective consumer—what good then is the research effort?

The following checklist for descriptive research will aid the researcher in his analytical efforts. Evaluate the article from 5 (excellent) to 0 (poor). Follow up by completing the Composite Score form and calculating an average score. The rating scale at the end of the Composite Score will provide a letter grade for the article under evaluation.

THE PROBLEM

The problem was clearly stated in theoretical terms.	Excellent 5 4 3 2 1 Poor
The problem was clearly stated in operational terms.	Excellent 5 4 3 2 1 Poor
The variables measured are clearly defined.	Excellent 5 4 3 2 1 Poor
External variables are identified and controlled.	Excellent 5 4 3 2 1 Poor
An appropriate basis was used in selection of the variables.	Excellent 5 4 3 2 1 Poor
A workable and verifiable hypothesis was formed.	Excellent 5 4 3 2 1 Poor
The hypothesis was an outgrowth of some theory or problem.	Excellent 5 4 3 2 1 Poor
Hypotheses were formed on the basis of empirical research.	Excellent 5 4 3 2 1 Poor

Score _____

DEVELOPMENT OF THE INSTRUMENT

Variables under observation are directly measurable.	Excellent 5 4 3 2 1 Poor
Criterion variables are realistic.	Excellent 5 4 3 2 1 Poor
Parameters for item selection were adequate.	Excellent 5 4 3 2 1 Poor
A pilot study was conducted to select items.	Excellent 5 4 3 2 1 Poor
Tests were run on item validity.	Excellent 5 4 3 2 1 Poor
The basis on which scales were selected is adequate.	Excellent 5 4 3 2 1 Poor
Error variance caused by response mechanisms is made clear.	Excellent 5 4 3 2 1 Poor
Error variance attributable to interaction among scale items is made explicit.	Excellent 5 4 3 2 1 Poor
Error variance caused by items is clear.	Excellent 5 4 3 2 1 Poor
Error caused by scales is stated clearly.	Excellent 5 4 3 2 1 Poor
A pilot was conducted to test instrumentation reliability.	Excellent 5 4 3 2 1 Poor
Validating keys are included in the study.	Excellent 5 4 3 2 1 Poor
Realiability measurements are sufficient.	Excellent 5 4 3 2 1 Poor

Score _____

THE DESIGN

The population is specified.	Excellent 5 4 3 2 1 Poor
Adequate sampling procedures were used.	Excellent 5 4 3 2 1 Poor
The sampling procedures were clear.	Excellent 5 4 3 2 1 Poor
The statistical model chosen to be used in the test is appropriate to the methodology, population, and hypotheses under consideration.	Excellent 5 4 3 2 1 Poor
The level of significance was stated and justified.	Excellent 5 4 3 2 1 Poor

Score _____

PROCEDURES

The study can be easily replicated.	Excellent 5 4 3 2 1 Poor
A sufficient sample was used.	Excellent 5 4 3 2 1 Poor
Directions are stated clearly on how the instrument is to be used.	Excellent 5 4 3 2 1 Poor
Working and word placement biases are identified.	Excellent 5 4 3 2 1 Poor
An 80 percent response was elicited from the population.	Excellent 5 4 3 2 1 Poor
Respondent characteristics are sufficient to justify analysis.	Excellent 5 4 3 2 1 Poor
Interview techniques and procedures were standardized.	Excellent 5 4 3 2 1 Poor
The strategy chosen for administering the instrument was selected for high yield returns.	Excellent 5 4 3 2 1 Poor
The grouping schemes used resulted from appropriate tests for validity and reliability.	Excellent 5 4 3 2 1 Poor
The study administered treatments to minimize extraneous sources of error.	Excellent 5 4 3 2 1 Poor

Score _____

ANALYSIS

The criterion measured was appropriate for the study's objectives.	Excellent 5 4 3 2 1 Poor
There was evidence of reliability of the criterion measured.	Excellent 5 4 3 2 1 Poor
The statistical assumptions for a valid test were satisfactory.	Excellent 5 4 3 2 1 Poor
The level of significance for the objectives was appropriate.	Excellent 5 4 3 2 1 Poor

Score _____

Summarize the evaluation as follows:

> The Problem . . . . Score _____
>
> Development of the Instrument . . . . Score _____
>
> The Design . . . . Score _____
>
> Procedures . . . . Score _____
>
> Analysis . . . . Score _____
>
> Total Score . . . . . _____ divided by 50 = _____

The following will serve as a basis for evaluation of the overall article. (Round off to the nearest whole number.)

> For a grade of A, 4 quality points
> For a grade of B, 3 quality points
> For a grade of C, 2 quality points
> For a grade of D, 1 quality point

FINDING INFORMATION

Most libraries in the United States utilize one of two systems for cataloging and classifying information. These are the Library of Congress Classification Scheme and the Dewey Decimal System. The Library of Congress uses the letters of the alphabet to identify certain fields of information. Utilized by most libraries having collections in excess of 25,000 volumes, this system is outlined below.

CLASSIFICATIONS IN THE
LIBRARY OF CONGRESS SYSTEM

A		General Works—Polygraphy
B		Philosophy, Religion, Psychology
C		History-Auxiliary Sciences
D		History and Topography
EF		American History
G		Geography, Anthropology
H		Social Sciences
I		Vacant
J		Political Science
K		Law
L		Education, General Works
	LA	History of Education
	LB	Theory of Education
	LC	Special Forms and Applications

	LD	US Universities and Colleges
	LE	American Education (Outside US)
	LG	Asia, Africa, Oceania
	LH	School Periodicals
	LI	Vacant
	LJ	Fraternities, Societies
	LT	Textbooks
M		Music
N		Fine Arts
O		Vacant
P		Language, Literature
Q		Science
R		Medicine
S		Agriculture
T		Technology
U		Military Science
V		Naval Science
W		Vacant
X		Vacant
Y		Vacant
Z		Library Science-Bibliography

Books in the library are cataloged by subject, title and author. Subject headings for the Library of Congress System are chosen from a book entitled *Library of Congress Subject Headings.* The following cards illustrate how cards would be placed in the card catalog for the book *Publishing and Bookselling; a History from the Earliest Time to the Present Day.*

Z Mumby, Frank Arthur, 1872-
323   Publishing and bookselling; a history from the earliest times to
M95 the present day. With a bibliography by W.H. Peet. [Further rev. ed.]
London, Cape [1954]

    438 p. illus. 23 cm

    First published in 1910 under title: The romance of book selling.

    1. Booksellers and bookselling--Gt. Brit. 2. Publishers and publishing--Gt. Brit. 3. Booksellers and bookselling--Bibl. 4. Publishers and publishing--Bibl. I. Title.

Z323.M95 1954   655.442   55-492

Library of Congress   [15]

BOOKSELLERS AND BOOKSELLING--GT. BRIT.

Z Mumby, Frank Arthur, 1872-
323   Publishing and bookselling; a history from the earliest times to
M95 the present day. With a bibliography by W.H. Peet. [Further rev. ed.]
London, Cape [1954]

438 p. illus. 23 cm

First published in 1910 under title: The romance of book selling.

1. Booksellers and bookselling--Gt. Brit. 2. Publishers and publishing--Gt. Brit. 3. Booksellers and bookselling--Bibl. 4. Publishers and publishing--Bibl. I. Title.

Z323.M95   1954   655.442   55-492

Library of Congress   [15]

Publishing and bookselling

Z Mumby, Frank Arthur, 1872-
323   Publishing and bookselling; a history from the earliest times
M95 to the present day. With a bibliography by W.H. Peet. [Further rev. ed.] London, Cape [1954]

438 p. illus. 23 cm

First published in 1910 under title: The romance of book selling.

1. Booksellers and bookselling--Gt. Brit. 2. Publishers and publishing--Gt. Brit. 3. Booksellers and bookselling--Bibl. 4. Publishers and publishing--Bibl. I. Title.

Z323.M95   1954   655.442   55-492

Library of Congress   [15]

The Dewey Decimal System

The Dewey Decimal System uses numbers to identify various fields of information. Used by many smaller libraries, this system is outlined below:

- 000   Generalities
- 100   Philosophy and related disciplines
- 200   Religion
- 300   The social sciences
- 400   Language
- 500   Pure sciences
- 600   Technology (applied sciences)
- 700   The arts
- 800   Literature (Belles-lettres)
- 900   General geography and history

The following cards illustrate the same book cataloged by subject, title and author. The only difference is the call number of the book. Subject headings for the Dewey Decimal System are chosen from Sears *List of Subject Headings*. In this instance the subject heading was identical with the Library of Congress heading. However, the two books do vary.

BOOKSELLERS AND BOOKSELLING--GT. BRIT.

655.442   Mumby, Frank Arthur, 1872-
M   Publishing and bookselling; a history from the earliest times to the present day. With a bibliography by W.H. Peet. [Further rev. ed.] London, Cape [1954]

   438 p. illus. 23 cm

   First published in 1910 under title: The romance of book selling.

   1. Booksellers and bookselling--Gt. Brit. 2. Publishers and publishing--Gt. Brit. 3. Booksellers and bookselling--Bibl. 4. Publishers and publishing--Bibl. I. Title.

   Z323.M95   1954   655.442   55-492

   Library of Congress   [15]

```
                    Publishing and bookselling
655.442    Mumby, Frank Arthur, 1872-
M                  Publishing and bookselling; a history from the earliest
           times to the present day. With a bibliography by W.H. Peet.
           [Further rev. ed.] London, Cape [1954]
                    438 p. illus. 23 cm.
                    First published in 1910 under title: The romance of
           book selling.
                    1. Booksellers and bookselling--Gt. Brit. 2. Publishers
           and publishing--Gt. Brit. 3. Booksellers and bookselling--Bibl.
           4. Publishers and publishing--Bibl. I. Title.
           Z323.M95      1954      655.442              55-492
           Library of Congress          [15]
```

```
655.442    Mumby, Frank Arthur, 1872-
                    Publishing and bookselling; a history from the earliest
           times to the present day. With a bibliography by W.H. Peet.
           [Further rev. ed.] London, Cape [1954]
                    438 p. illus. 23 cm.
                    First published in 1910 under title: The romance of
           book selling.
                    1. Booksellers and bookselling--Gt. Brit. 2. Publishers
           and publishing--Gt. Brit. 3. Booksellers and bookselling--Bibl.
           4. Publishers and publishing--Bibl. I. Title.
           Z323.M95      1954      655.442              55-492
           Library of Congress          [15]
```

ORGANIZING THE INFORMATION CENTER

If successful, a search of the literature for information about a subject results in a need to record it, organize it, and report it. While in the library, much can be done to facilitate these tasks by structuring the recording of the information when it is first written down. What information is actually recorded is determined by purpose or need. Since our discussion is directed toward research, this section will discuss gathering background information for research studies—other purposes will, in most instances, follow similar procedures but different information will be recorded.

Use of Cards

The first requirement for data recording is something on which to record. Information should always be recorded on bibliographical cards. Do not try to beat the system by using the back of envelopes, sheets of wrapping paper, or even newly acquired notebooks and/or paper from the bookstore—use cards. The cards allow much more flexibility in arranging the material into meaningful form and for developing a narrative report. The size of the card is not crucial, but 4 by 6 is usually considered minimum, and 5 by 8 is more commonly used. If one tends to write quite a bit about each source, the larger cards will prevent the use of more than one card for an entry.

Information for the Card

The card should first have a complete bibliographic entry for the item as it is to appear in a bibliography later. The student must decide (with the help or any regulations that apply to selection) what form the final bibliography will be in (i.e., APA, Campbell, Turabian, Dugdale) and learn that form. The example in Figure 12 is in Campbell's form. Other styles may vary, but in general they include the same information. For a book: (1) author or publishing agent; (2) complete title; (3) place of publication; (4) publisher; and (5) date of publication.

Additional information can be recorded on the card as required. The information to be written is selected for its significance to the investigation. Generally, it will be (1) a quotation, (2) a paraphrase, or (3) a summary. If a direct quotation is recorded, it should be indicated by quotation marks. Record the page number since it is needed in the footnote for a direct quotation, a paraphrase, and a summary. Direct quotations are discouraged in final writing, but a direct quotation on a card can be used as such if the meaning is lost in a paraphrase.

The record of research study information should include as a minimum the following additional information.

1. Purpose of the study, including the question asked and the hypothesis.
2. Research method used (historical, descriptive, or experimental).
3. Type of data used (test scores, judges' ratings, and so on).
4. Statistic used (i.e., chi square, median test).
5. Results and researcher's conclusions.
6. Personal reaction.
7. Any other information that the investigator determines important.

NOTES ON NOTETAKING CENTER

1. Use cards. One note to a card. 4 × 6 cards are easy to handle. 5 × 8 cards allow for more narrative.
2. Write the bibliographical entry and library call numbers at the top of the note card.
3. Classify cards by subject heading. Color code edges on cards to help find material for the final writing.
4. Be sure that each note is written clearly and completely in a manner in which it can be understood when needed. Do not plan to recopy because this introduces a chance for error. Use a typewriter if possible.
5. Develop skill in paraphrasing so that the original meaning remains, but is in your own words. Identify clearly all direct quotations and record the page number.
6. Develop a filing system for all notes. Find a secure place and file the notes as soon as they are made. If they must be carried about, an accordion folder with your name and address on it is a convenient way to carry them.

EDUCATION RESOURCES INFORMATION CENTERS (ERIC)

ERIC is a nationwide information network designed and developed by the U.S. Office of Education, and now operated by the National Institute of Education. It consists of a coordinating stall in Washington, D.C., and sixteen specialized clearinghouses, located at universities or with professional organizations across the country. ERIC clearinghouses monitor and acquire current significant information relevant to education. Information is indexed and the material is made available to the public in a number of ways. The type of material made available are reports of innovative programs, conference proceedings, bibliographies, outstanding professional papers, curriculum-related materials, and educational research and development reports. These are called ERIC documents.

The index section to ERIC is compiled semiannually and annually. Additionally, two cumulative volumes cover a span of several years, one volume covering 1966 through 1969, and the other covering 1970 through 1971. To search a given topic it is not necessary to consult monthly issues of ERIC for those periods covered by the cumulative indexes. However, the monthly issues are necessary to locate the most recent material which has not been cumulated. The following steps are necessary in an ERIC search:

1. Establishing a clear and concise statement of the problem or information needed. This should include the major topical areas,

specific subtopics, and information sought (e.g., research, methodology, bibliography, summary review, or other).
2. Determining the descriptors or subject terms by using the *Thesaurus of ERIC Descriptors.*
3. Using the latest cumulated issue of the indexes of ERIC, searching the subject indexes for the descriptors that are chosen. This procedure also includes listing the ED number in columns under each descriptor.
4. Going to the document resumé section of RIE to search for the ED numbers, to evaluate the resumés, and to note those that appear to satisfy the search goal.
5. Finding the reports in the microfiche files for those documents that were selected from the resumés and viewing the reports on a microfiche reader.

Often students using ERIC are uncertain what subject terms to use for locating material on their topic. For instance, someone doing research on "gifted students" would not find that term listed in the indexes and might conclude that no materials were available. To avoid confusion, the student should begin his search by consulting the *Thesaurus of ERIC Descriptors,* an authority list of, and a cross reference guide to, the subject headings used in the various ERIC indexes. The *Thesaurus of ERIC Descriptors* serves two important functions by directing the researcher to the correct term for locating material on a topic, and by providing cross references to additional terms which relate to the topic.

For example, if the student looks up the term "gifted students" in the *Thesaurus,* he will be instructed to use the term "gifted" instead. Under the term "gifted," the *Thesaurus* lists broader terms (BT), related terms (RT), and used for (UF). The *Thesaurus* also uses the abbreviations SN (scope note) which defines the use of the term in the ERIC system, and NT (narrower terms). These aids will reveal additional material if searched in the indexes. They also help narrow terms.

The most comprehensive index of documenting an ERIC microfiche is called *Resources in Education* (RIE). RIE is issued monthly, corresponding to the monthly shipments of documents. The first section of each monthly issue consists of an abstract or resumé for each document issued that month, arranged by ED number. Abstracts are grouped by clearinghouse, being arranged in alphabetical order according to the initials signifying a specific clearinghouse (e.g., SE-Science, Mathematics and Environmental Education). It is worth noting that the same abstract found in RIE may also be found in two other places: (1) on the first page of the document itself and (2) in cumulative volumes called *ERIC*. The second section of RIE consists of various indexes—subject, author and institution. Under each subject heading or descriptors, appropriate report titles and their ED numbers are listed.

Current Index to Journals in Education (CIJE) is a companion publication to RIE. CIJE is a monthly publication, covering more than 700 journals and periodicals related to education, representing the core periodical literature in the field.

Articles listed in CIJE are processed by the ERIC Clearinghouse and Macmillan Information. A CIJE search is conducted similar to a search conducted in RIE; the contents of each issue of CIJE are arranged in terms of numerical EJ (Educational Journal) order and division by clearinghouse.

Some of the articles identified in CIJE have brief annotations describing the articles's contents, and the remainder have descriptive terms. From these terms and the article title, the reader is able to obtain adequate information concerning the article's content. A judgment concerning its usefulness for his purposes can then be made. Articles which have annotations also have a listing of descriptive terms.

CIJE issues contain a subject index and an author index. Each issue also contains a "journal contents" index which lists journals and the articles from each journal which are included.

Certain microfiche are absent because some items listed in the indexes have not been reproduced on microfiche. Typically, items not on microfiche are copyrighted and may be secured through other sources. If a document is missing from the files, consult its resume.́ If the document was not reproduced on ERIC microfiche, the resume' will include the note, "Not available from EDRS." EDRS stands for ERIC Documents Reproduction Service.

It is important to reiterate three procedures in using ERIC:

1. If in doubt about what term to use, consult the *Thesaurus of ERIC Descriptors* to establish the correct subject heading before proceeding to the indexes.
2. Use the cumulative index for those years which are complete rather than searching monthly issues of *Resources in Education.* Consult monthly issues for the most recent materials.
3. If a document is absent from the microfiche files, locate its resume' to determine if it is one of those **not** available from EDRS.

Another useful tool for discovering what research has previously been conducted on a subject is the *Encyclopedia of Educational Research a Project of the American Educational Association,* ed. by Chester W. Harris, with the assistance of Marie R. Liba. This is not an encyclopedia in the usual sense. This work aims to evaluate and put into perspective the findings of educational research. Arrangement is alphabetical by subject and articles are signed and dated.

Educational Index is an author and subject index to the contents of approximately 223 educational periodicals, proceedings, yearbooks, bulletins, and monographic series include administration, preschool, elementary, secondary, higher, and adult education, teacher education, counseling and guidance, curriculum and curriculum materials. Subject fields indexed include the arts, applied science and technology, audiovisual education, business education, comparative and international education, exceptional children and special education, health and physical education, languages and linguistics, mathematics psychology and mental health, religious education, social studies, and educational research relative to areas and fields indexed. *Education Index* is published monthly from September through June, with permanent bound annual cumulations.

The *United States Government Publications: Monthly Catalog* is a current bibliography of publications issued by all branches of the national government. General instructions for ordering and a list of documents published during the month are arranged by department and bureau, with indication for each publication of its full title, date, paging, and price.

SUMMARY

Closely related to answering questions is the storage of the answers. Most information is to be found in libraries, making them an integral part of the research process. Researchers use libraries primarily to gather information about the field being studied, knowing that valid research is based on their knowing as much as they can about closely related topics. Skillful use of the library requires (1) an overall understanding of its organization, and (2) knowledge of reference materials—indexes, guides, and such—to uncover the needed information.

Indexes for the library have been presented to familiarize the reader with a way of quickly locating possible needed information. In addition to the card catalogue that lists most materials except periodical articles, the *Readers' Guide to Periodical Literature, Education Index, and Current Index to Journals in Education* are all used to give complete coverage to educational information. Other aids to library searches have been included.

Information should be recorded on 4 × 6 or 5 × 8 cards, and should include a complete bibliography entry, plus pertinent information. For reporting about research the information should include the purpose of the study, type of research, kind of data, statistics used, results, conclusions, and a reaction statement.

Chapter 2 will deal with the theoretical development of personality and how this relates to the teacher-student learning relationships.

Chapter 2
PERSONALITY THEORIES

Personality is generally attributed to human beings for three major reasons: (1) each individual is unique in behavior, yet at the same time similar to other humans; (2) individuals can change behavior; and (3) there is a certain amount of consistency to the individual's behavior (Baughman, 1972). This means that although each person is different from all other persons, there are certain commonalities to being human, that personalities are not rigid and fixed at any one stage in life, yet there is enough consistency to the individual behavior patterns to allow predictability.

The study of personality can be thought of as the study of individual differences. It is the responsibility of the teacher to observe the behavior of the students with some degree of sophistication so that he will be able to make some educated guesses in interpretation, to formulate hypotheses, and to predict the future behavior of the students. A major task of the teacher is to promote the development of healthy personalities. The focal point of this chapter, then, is the development of personality within the individual.

McNeil (1974, p. 83) has described personality as "the pattern of characteristic ways of behaving and thinking that make up the individual's style of adjusting to his environment." This definition seems adequate for purposes of the present study. Personality may be looked at from three theoretical frames of reference—psychoanalytic, humanistic, and learning theory. First, it is necessary to explain what a theory is, and to define frame of reference. A theory attempts to organize a set of ideas, assumptions, or hypotheses into some kind of logical form. "Frame of reference" means a set of related concepts which make up a somewhat systematic approach to the study of certain problems. For example, using the behavioral frame of reference in observing and interpreting behavior means focusing attention on certain behavioral categories.

PSYCHOANALYTIC THEORY

Sigmund Freud formulated the most complete of all personality theories. He was the first theorist to stress the developmental aspects, emphasizing the importance of infancy and childhood in the formulation of personality.

Freud saw man as being caught between "life instincts" and "death instincts:" this results in a never ending struggle between inner forces (drives) until the inevitable end—death wins out. Freud believed that a great amount of a person's behavior is directed by what he termed "unconscious mental processes." The material in the unconscious is constantly pushing to come into awareness, while other forces in the personality are attempting to keep these processes unconscious. The result may be an experiencing of inner conflict which the person cannot explain. Energy used to keep the unconscious processes repressed is not available to the individual for other purposes; this limits his productivity. Freud gave primary emphasis to unconscious mental processes in his dynamic personality theory.

Structure of Personality

Freud emphasized conflict between forces in the personality. He maintained that the structure of personality contained three subsystems—the id, ego, and superego—and attempted to explain personality in terms of the interactions of these systems of psychic function. The id, according to Freud, consists of everything psychological that is inherited; it contains the basic biological urges of hunger, sex, thirst and other needs which have motivational properties; it furnishes all of the psychic energy for the operation of the other two systems in the ego and the superego; it operates on the pleasure principle, and usually at an unconscious level. Throughout life the id continues to play an active role, however, it is highly controlled by the second system of personality, the ego.

The ego is considered to be the executive part of the personality, directing and controlling the id by insisting that needs be met through socially acceptable behaviors. The ego is controlled by the reality principle and adjusts behavior so that it is appropriate to the situation. Further, the ego serves as an integrating force for the conflicting demands of the id, the superego, and the outside world. However, the ego exists to gratify the drives of the id and not to frustrate them. The ego's power is derived from the id and its primary function is that of mediating between the biological needs of the individual and the prevailing situations and conditions within the environment in order to sustain life and the survival of the species.

The third system of personality, the superego, develops out of the ego. It represents the traditional values of society. Parents and other highly important people in the life of the child influence the child's learning of these values and ideals through the use of rewards and punishments. The superego is thought to be the moral part of the self.

Freud suggested that there are two components of the superego, the ego-ideal and the conscience. The ego-ideal represents the person one would like to be. Whatever the parents approve of and reward the child for doing becomes incorporated into his ego-ideal; whatever the parents punish the child for doing tends to become incorporated into the conscience. Subsequently, the conscience causes guilt feelings when the child does not live up to his ego-ideal, and the ego-ideal rewards the person when he does measure up to these standards by making him feel proud of himself. Hence, it is through this process of rewards and punishments that the child's self-control is substituted for parental and/or outside control.

In summary, a person's behavior represents a compromise among the demands of these three different sources: the id, the superego, and the external world. For effective behavior and a healthy personality, the person cannot ignore basic drives (id), the ideals and standards of conduct developed by the individual (superego), nor the world of reality outside self. The function of the ego then is to integrate the individual's behavior so that it is in harmony with the differing demands.

Psychosexual Stages of Development

Human psychopathy results from early traumatic experiences and frustrations. The particular emotional disorder that will appear depends on the time in life when the trauma occurs and the number of positive experiences that the individual has to help compensate for the frustrations and anxieties. Freud identified a set of anxieties that result from the conflicts experienced by the individual during each stage of development. These stages of development Freud labeled the *oral, anal, phallic, latency* and *genital* stages.

According to Freud, the first five years of life are of extreme importance in terms of the development of personality. Freud attached great significance to the role that sexual urges play. In fact, he defined the stages of development during these early years in terms of a mode of reaction of a particular zone of the body. The principal region of activity for the oral stage Freud identified as the mouth; the second stage, the anal, starts about the second year and continues until about the 3rd or 4th year. In the anal stage the infant derives satisfaction through the eliminative processes. The third stage is called the phallic stage in which the sex organs become the main erogenous zones. These three stages constitute the pregenital stages.

Next, the child goes into the latency stage which Freud referred to as a quiet period in which the impulses are held in a state of repression. The final stage is the genital stage during which adolescence reactivates the sexual impulses. The ego's task is to see that these impulses are properly sublimated and that appropriate substitutions are found so that the individual can move smoothly into a level of maturity characterized by a healthy heterosexual relationship with a member of the opposite sex.

Freud believed that the way in which sexual urges are handled influence the total psychological makeup of the growing child. Psychological development is like biological growth in that it takes place regardless of the specific environmental conditions that may exist for the individual. The child must go through each successive psychosexual stage of development and somehow learn to cope with the problems that arise in each stage; this adjustment process affects, in turn, how the individual will adjust in the next stage of development. Inability to cope in one stage hampers adjustment in the successive stages. Likewise, successful coping within each stage enhances the adjustments in the adult.

Defense Mechanisms

Another of Freud's most important contributions is the concept of defense mechanisms. Freud believed that "personality develops in response to four major sources of tension: (1) physiological growth processes, (2) frustration, (3) conflicts, and (4) threats (Hall and Lindzey, 1970, p. 45)." A person who is threatened experiences fear or anxiety. Then the person takes steps to avoid this emotional state, thereby establishing defense mechanisms. Freud stressed the avoidance of pain as a central factor in directing the person's behavior, or perhaps even the principal motive for defense mechanisms.

Defense mechanisms are parts of the ego but cannot be understood without knowledge of the id and superego, or for that matter, knowledge of the psychosexual stages of development. In the early stages of the child's life, other people are the main source of pain. However, with the emergence of the superego, the child can inflict punishment on self. This means there are two sources of threat, an external source and an internal source. Freud maintained that the person's basic fear is that he will not be able to control his impulses, and, as a consequence, is afraid of punishment, either external or internal (Baughman, 1972). The person is rarely even faintly aware of these urges; therefore, Freud believed that defense mechanisms are established, for the most part, at an unconscious level. Defense mechanisms are attempts to distort reality, yet they are necessary adjustment mechanisms. When used excessively, however, they may present psychological problems to the individual. It would be well now to look at several of the major defense mechanisms.

Regression

As the person goes through the psychosexual stages of development he is moving toward maturity if all goes well. However, a person may not move from one stage but may remain at that level of development which is called fixation, or the person may move backward to an earlier phase of development which is called regression. An example might be a second grader who suddenly reverts to thumb sucking as a result of a traumatic experience at home.

Repression is the pushing into the unconscious of painful impulses or experiences. However, the impulse does not cease to exist simply because it is pushed aside, but will constantly strive to get into a conscious level of awareness. In this way the ego must use energy to keep the material repressed. Perhaps repression is the most dangerous of all the defense mechanisms simply because the impulses are at an unconscious level, and the person cannot deal with them at will. The person may be unaware of the repressed material even though this material influences his behavior (Baughman, 1972).

Projection usually involves failure to recognize a characteristic as being one's own, and attributing this characteristic to another person. A person who dislikes his teacher may say, "The teacher hates me," thereby attributing the undesirable feeling of hate to the teacher. This may also be an attempt to downgrade the other person while seeking to enhance self.

Reaction formation is the expression of behavior opposite to the repressed personality tendency. This may manifest itself in an extreme such as a mother constantly expressing affection for her child with excessive attentiveness when, in reality, she does not want the child.

Introjection is simply to take on characteristics of others—or the individual may develop an *identification* with the person whom he admires and, as a consequence, may take on some of that person's personality characteristics.

Rationalization means to offer an explanation for some behavior that the person is experiencing conflict over. The explanation is not accurate and is an attempt to disguise the real reason for the conflict.

USING PSYCHOANALYTIC CONCEPTS IN THE CLASSROOM

Through a knowledge of some of the basic psychoanalytic concepts the teacher can broaden his perspective in understanding the child:

1. The importance of early childhood experiences is stressed.
2. Through knowledge of the developmental history of the child the teacher can be in a position to deal with some of the personality conflicts that are direct results of early experiences.
3. The importance of the overall adjustment of the child is emphasized. The teacher should concentrate more on total adjustment than on specific behaviors.
4. Unconscious motivation plays a big part in personality.
5. Through understanding of the individual's use of particular defense mechanisms the teacher can get a better picture of the person's ego, the nature of his drives (id), and his value system (superego). In fact, this may be the beginning of the teacher's understanding of the student's total personality.

HUMANISTIC THEORIES OF PERSONALITY

Humanistic psychology is considered to be a "third force" in psychology, with psychoanalytic and behaviorism the other two. It is the uniqueness of each person, his values and worth as an individual, that is important to the humanistic frame of reference. According to Bugental (1967, p. 7), ". . . humanistic psychology has as its ultimate goal the preparation of a complete description of what it means to be alive as a human being. This would include an inventory of man's native endowment; his growth, evolution and decline; his interactions with various environing conditions; . . . the range and variety of experience possible to him; and his meaningful place in the universe."

Two personality theories that embrace the humanistic school of thought include Abraham Maslow's holistic-dynamic theory and Carl Rogers' self theory. A brief description of these two theories will be helpful.

Maslow's Holistic-dynamic Theory

Maslow felt that psychology has dwelled more on man's frailties than upon his strengths, that psychologists have looked at life in terms of avoiding pain rather than in taking action to gain happiness and joy. Maslow attempted to give a portrait of the "whole man," which includes love and well-being. Maslow wrote (1967) that ". . . in practically every human being there is an active will toward health, an impulse towards growth, or towards the actualization of human potential."

Maslow emphasized that as the individual grows and matures in a healthy and reinforcing environment there is an active effort on the part of the person to realize his nature, and the creative powers within the person manifest themselves. When the individual is neurotic or unhappy, it is because of his environment, or because of his own distorted thinking. The individual becomes destructive when his nature is denied or frustrated (see Chapter 3, p. 33).

Maslow's theory is one of human motivation. There is a struggle to satisfy the basic physiological and safety needs before the individual is free to handle the needs of belongingness, love, and self-esteem. Maslow arranged these needs in hierarchical order according to potency. Each of the basic needs must be satisfied at least to some degree before the individual is free to move up the hierarchical ladder—on to the ultimate goal of self-actualization.

Maslow studied healthy and creative persons while formulating ideas about personality into some kind of theoretical framework. As a matter of fact, Maslow made an intensive study of a group of people whom he considered to be self-actualizing—that is, realizing their potentialities to the fullest.

Self-theory

Carl Rogers is closely identified with humanistic psychology. The self is one of the central constructs in Roger's theory. The self is subject to strong influences from the environment, particularly the social environment. Rogers does not focus on stages of development as Freud does, but emphasizes instead the ways in which evaluations of the individual by others during childhood influences the development of personality. Of particular significance to Rogers' theory is how the individual perceives his own self. In this case, Rogers is using self to refer to the total personality.

As the child grows and develops he learns to play many roles, such as teacher, parent, doctor, etc. The child learns to distinguish between and among the various behaviors required for each role; a continuous sense of identity is present regardless of the role being accepted by the child at any given time. The developing self-concept provides flexibility to change behavior when the person shifts roles.

To the person, the self is the core of significant aspects in the environment. However, the self extends and encompasses other objects and events beyond the physical being. For example, extensions of the self may include the entire family, community, state, country, etc. Another child, or the teacher, may cause bad feelings if he says anything derogatory about any part of the self (extensions) of the child.

The Development of the Self-concept

The self-concept develops out of the child's many training experiences. During the preverbal period, the child learns to separate his physical body from the rest of the world, and this becomes the body image. Secondly, the young child seems to form a core of a self-concept which can be detected by his expression of delight after an accomplishment (i.e., taking the first step or saying a word). The individual strives to be competent. Thirdly, the growing child learns not only to perceive self but how to value self while interacting with the important people in the child's life, such as parents. How these persons respond to the child is crucial. The child is continually watching others for feedback about self. This feedback lets the child know if he is a person of worth who deserves love, or if the child is not worthy. Sometimes parents and teachers let their own problems interfere with child training and do not consider the effects of their behavior on the child's developing self-concept.

Through experiences with others the child also learns what he should be—the self-ideal. Later, as the child grows and matures, it is this discrepancy between the self and the self-ideal that causes many problems. When the person does not live up to his own self-ideal, the individual experiences guilt and conflict. Rogers maintains that if the evaluations by others of the growing child were exclusively positive no incongruity would occur, and the child would learn to be psychologically adjusted, and therefore fully functioning.

Rogers believes that within each person there is a basic tendency and striving for growth to actualize and enhance the self; if given a nonthreatening environment, the individual will choose to grow.

USING HUMANISTIC PSYCHOLOGY IN THE CLASSROOM

1. It is necessary to work with and to understand the whole child, which includes a need for love and well-being.
2. Knowledge of human motivation in terms of needs will give the teacher insight as to developing readiness for learning.
3. A positive and reinforcing classroom climate is most conducive to learning.
4. Knowledge of how the child develops a self-concept can help the teacher in many ways to:
    a. provide opportunities for role playing
    b. practice giving positive feedback to students
    c. provide success experiences for all students
    d. be alert to how the student perceives the classroom situation, and how the student sees self.

LEARNING THEORIES

Learning theorists have attempted to find relationships between stimulus condition and behavior. For a discussion of learning theories as they relate to personality theory, the student should turn to Chapter 5.

SUMMARY

This chapter dealt with an analysis of two major personality theoretical orientations. In psychoanalytic theory, the structure of personality, stages of development, and defense mechanisms were discussed. Within the humanistic frame of reference, Maslow's holistic-dynamic theory and Roger's self-theory were explored. Implications for both orientations were given for classroom use.

Chapter 3 is concerned with the interaction of hereditary and cultural variables as they influence the development of personality.

PERSONALITY THEORIES
STUDENT OBJECTIVES

In an objective type test which may include matching, multiple choice, and short answers, the student will be able to:

- (K) 1. Know the three major reasons personality is attributed to human beings.
- (An) 2. Differentiate between the three personality theories.
- (K) 3. List the three theoretical frames of reference.
- (An) 4. Distinguish between the levels of psychosexual development.
- (C) 5. Explain the three subsystems of the structure of personality according to Freud.
- (K) 6. Identify the two components of the superego.
- (Ap) 7. Apply the defense mechanisms used when presented with various examples.
- (K) 8. Know the principal motive for defense mechanism.
- (K) 9. Know the most dangerous defense mechanism and defend this position.
- (Ap) 10. Differentiate between the uses of humanistic and psychoanalytic concepts used by teachers in the classroom.
- (K) 11. State the four major sources of tension that cause personality to develop.
- (C) 12. Explain the two forces that Freud saw in a never ending struggle.
- (An) 13. Organize Maslow's theory of needs in hierarchical order.
- (S) 14. Compare the humanistic and psychoanalytic approaches and list the advantages of each.
- (E) 15. Evaluate an article on either the psychoanalytic or humanistic approach to personality.

Chapter 3
THE DEVELOPMENT OF PERSONALITY

The brief overview of personality theory in Chapter 2 has shown a great deal of variation and diversity among the leading theorists. However, looking at personality from either of the three major approaches, it is clear that the theorists agree on one fact—personality development. This chapter will study personality within a developmental perspective. The focus is on change—psychological changes that occur with increasing chronological age and the complex interaction of biological and environmental factors.

The teacher attempts to influence the student's developmental process by selecting and setting up experiences that are appropriate to the developmental level of the child. This developmental status is determined by both constitutional (hereditary) and environmental (cultural) variables. It would be well first to examine the biological or constitutional determinants of development.

HEREDITY

Chromosomes contain the necessary mechanisms of heredity. Thousands of chemical units known as genes are contained in the chromosomes. Genes are the bearers of heredity. At conception the fetus receives 46 chromosomes, 23 from each parent, which represent the individual's hereditary potential. The number of different possible combinations from these genes is beyond imagination. Similarities, as well as individual differences, are insured because no chromosomes are in the zygote (fertilized egg) except those that were contributed by the two parents. Although each gene takes its place in inheritance, the combination of many genes is required to produce a single inherited trait.

In 1962, J.D. Watson, F.H.C. Crick and M.H.F. Wilkins came up with an explanation of the series of genetic events; they deciphered the molecular structure of the chemical that makes up genetic material, DNA (deoxyribonucleic acid). The DNA Code carries information to direct the cell's manufacture of proteins, and ultimately the beginning of life in the human being.

Only physiological characteristics are generally considered to be inherited—color of hair, skin, eyes, body structure, blood type, color blindness, blood pressure, allergies, etc. Other characteristics are attributed to a combination of heredity and environment. These include mentality, health, susceptibility and immunity from certain diseases. Acquired characteristics are not inherited. For example, morality or immorality is not inherited. Nevertheless, these acquired characteristics may influence the development of the child because of the family environment.

Individuals are born with temperaments, not personalities. This temperament (temperamental disposition) represents the core of personality, and develops into personality as the infant, and later the child, interacts with the outside world.

Environmental factors can alter genetically based patterns of behavior. Studies have shown that each infant is born with his own behavior patterns, unlike those of all other infants. One baby may seldom cry, while another cries incessantly. Still another infant may demand attention while another seems content to be left alone. These observations have led researchers to believe that infants are born with different temperaments, and that these differences affect their personality development.

Maturation

Developmental changes that are due to heredity occur within the child as time passes if the child's environment is supportive of development. The child grows larger; the functioning of the endocrine glands changes; increasing amounts of sex hormones and adrenal androgens are produced during adolescence which stimulate the reproductive organs to develop. Environments that are deficient in certain ways may prohibit maturation and growth, and as a consequence, the development of the individual. Lack of proper diet and other severe deprivations are examples.

Basically, there are three views of development: maturational, environmental, and cognitive developmental (Wiggins et al., 1976). Maturational theories emphasize unfolding maturational stages in which order, timing and patterning of their development is encoded into the genotype. Environmental theories assume that mental structures are a result of outside events. Cognitive developmental theory maintains that personality results from the interaction of certain structuring tendencies within the organism with the structure of the external world, which is essentially the position taken by the present authors.

Primary Needs

Infants are born with certain needs, and much of the interaction with the infant is determined by the adults satisfying these needs. How the adults (mother, father, babysitter, etc.) go about taking care of the infant's basic needs is of crucial importance in determining how the infant's personality will develop.

The primary needs are based on biological properties that are common to all human beings. They are not a result of learning. Primary needs include hunger, thirst, a need to eliminate, to breathe, etc. Some evidence indicates that the primary needs have differential strength from infant to infant. An infant's behavior may indicate that he has an active need, even though the caretaker (mother, father, or other person) may not know exactly what the need is. Crying and restless movements are expressions of many of the infant's primary needs; these movements usually bring a concerned adult to investigate and take care of the infant's needs.

Through the gratification and frustration of primary needs, the infant begins to develop a conception of the outside world and of himself as a part of it. Through the infant's interaction with others in the process of having his needs satisfied, his personality begins to develop. If the adult taking care of the infant is generally pleasant, loving, and accepts all of the infant's behavior related to needs as natural, the infant will learn that these needs are natural situations and will not attach undue significance to them. On the other hand, if the adult ministering to the child's needs shows and expresses emotional stress, the infant will learn to be anxious and will generalize from the frustrated satisfaction of the primary needs to the secondary needs. Through learning, a great amount of variability develops from individual to individual due to the way primary needs are fulfilled.

Secondary Needs

Human behaviors include goals and incentives whose relations to primary needs may seem remote. Individuals strive for many different goals, such as status, power, competence, creativity, self-actualization, etc. These may be classified as secondary needs.

Secondary needs develop as the result of the child's experiences and they depend on learning. Many psychologist's argue that secondary needs develop from the primary needs. Whether primary or secondary, needs have motivational properties, and can often be used to explain why a person behaves in a certain way. Secondary needs develop throughout life, and the possibilities may be almost limitless. Nevertheless, all humans have similar biological structures and share a common culture.

CULTURAL INFLUENCE ON DEVELOPMENT

The culture includes all the learned behaviors that are shared by most of the members of a society and are handed down from one generation to another. However, religion, ethics, family structure, social class stratification, language, morals, laws, etc., vary from one culture to another.

Cultural Norms

Cultural norms serve as standards for evaluating conduct, personality, and even physical appearance. In contemporary society, a certain body build is favored for males and another for females. Deviation from these norms is frowned upon and affects the developing personality of the child. Culture helps to shape the life-style of the growing child; the parents teach the child the traditions within the culture. The culture certainly helps determine the early childhood experiences. At this point it would be fruitful to study the family as a unit within the culture.

Family Influences on Personality Development

A major responsibility of the family is to socialize the child. By this it is meant that the family teaches the child how to behave so as to "fit" into the family and the larger culture to which the family belongs (Baughman, 1972). The family is directly responsible for teaching the young how to control innate feelings and tendencies and how to express these in an acceptable manner. The child-training practices within a family are related to religion, social class, neighborhood, sex, and race. For instance, a child reared in an upper-class home in a suburban neighborhood may be exposed to a different set of rules to live by than the black child raised in an urban ghetto. Likewise, children of different sexes within the same family often experience two quite different sets of rules or standards.

Beginning with different clothes and colors for the newborn infant, parents treat boys and girls differently. Girls are handled tenderly and are generally given more love and affection, while boys are expected to be independent and tough. Boys are allowed to show aggression toward their parents and toward other children; girls are rewarded for repressing aggressive feelings. Parents expect the females to show more dependency needs than the male children. Some parents today are questioning this role differentiation and are attempting to bring their expectations of the male and female children closer together, hoping for optimum development where the individuals are freer to be themselves and not have to live up to these traditional sex-role expectations.

Other Subgroup Memberships

Each individual belongs to many subgroups, such as clubs and groups related to occupations, religion, social class, etc. Each group has and maintains its own set of behavioral norms. There is generally a well-developed system of social sanctions whereby individuals are rewarded and punished in accordance with their abiding by the group norms. Belonging to several groups contributes to individual differences. However, differences in the social norms of the various groups may cause conflict within individuals, such as the developing child seeing differences between the family's norms and those of another group to which he belongs—for example, a club whose members are mostly peers.

Role and Status of the Individual

Individuals play many different roles in the course of their lives—the student may assume the roles of student, son, daughter, sister, brother, etc. Some students accept their roles without conflict; others cannot. Each role has a certain status attached to it (Loree, 1970).

Sex-role stereotypes are widely shared within a particular culture. These are global ideas about so-called "masculine" and "feminine" traits that are generally based on average differences between the sexes. A boy growing up in our country is supposed to do certain kinds of things—climb trees, play football, enjoy the outdoors, and get dirty—while the girl plays with dolls, and helps mom around the house. These sex stereotypes serve as standards for judging self and others. However, within any subculture children vary in the degree to which they adopt sanctioned sex-roles. Children, girls in particular, from homes and schools where individualized development is emphasized do not adhere to the conventional sex-role standards as much as children from the more traditional backgrounds (Minuchin, 1965).

The School

The school is generally given the responsibility to see that the development of the child's cognitive and intellectual skills take place. However, any experienced teacher knows that much more takes place in the school than simple intellective functioning. Many of the child's experiences within the school influence behaviors that are certainly not considered to be of an intellectual character. It is important, therefore, for the school to create experiences for the students that will contribute toward the best possible development of their total behavior patterns and personality.

Social Structure of Classrooms

Each classroom has a social structure of its own. If the teacher is sensitive to this social structure it can be used to great advantage. Most students are aware of the particular social structure of any given class; this gives them information about themselves. The student's place within this structure is highly important. If the student sees self as having a high status position in the prestige system of the classroom structure, this student is far more likely to perform at a higher level intellectually than the student who sees self as having low status or as being an isolate. The teacher can manipulate the subgroup memberships within the classroom so as to give opportunities for developing social and interpersonal skills.

Too often the teacher, who is usually middle class, tends to favor the middle-class students since their values are similar to the teacher's. The teacher fails to recognize this favoritism as perpetuating the social class structure, when, indeed, it is the responsibility of the teacher to work with the lower-class children as well as the middle and upper classes and to attempt to build up self-esteem and status. Teacher responses to the individual student provide information about the student's worth.

Sex-typing in the School

Teachers, along with other important persons in the child's life, reward sex-appropriate behaviors. The teacher may encourage the males to be more self-reliant and achievement oriented and reward the females for obedience, nurturance and the demonstration of responsibility. The textbooks used in the schools often depict girls in a submissive role, either doing housework with mother, or playing with dolls. On the other hand, boys are usually pictured as outgoing, working with tools, or outdoors with dad, and in roles requiring physical activities. A widespread attempt is being made throughout the United States to make some changes in this respect. Many textbook companies are working aggressively to change these sex-role stereotype images, especially at the elementary school level where the personality of the developing child is subject to such great influence.

Socialization

The teacher has direct responsibility to help the child in the process of becoming socialized—to get along with others—to make social adjustments. Learning skills, such as physical or artistic activities, is important in gaining status from peers. The teacher should work toward helping each child become competent in some area. This in turn will help the individual student to gain the peer approval which seems to be a common need for both elementary school children and adolescents.

EMOTIONAL DEVELOPMENT

The subjective experience of emotion (from anxiety, anger, grief, joy, etc.) is learned. We learn which stimuli are appropriate for which emotions. For the infant, there is no gradation in emotional responses. However, as time goes on, the young child begins to distinguish between minor and major frustrations, and his responses soon become appropriate for the stimulus. The gradual change from a general gross expression of the child's emotions to a more individual and refined expression points up the effects of training by others and the subsequent control of self. Soon the child's increasing intellectual functioning helps him to analyze the experience of anger or fear (or whatever emotion) as soon as the cause is removed.

There are two possibilities open to the teacher to modify emotional behavior: (1) the child's perception of emotion-provoking situations can be changed, and (2) the child's overt response to the experienced emotion can be modified (Loree, 1970, p. 81). The teacher may help the child to overcome fear by allowing the child to come in contact with the fear-provoking object with no unpleasant consequences. Or, to exemplify number 2 above, the child can be taught to substitute one response to anger for another, i.e., express anger verbally rather than through physical aggression.

The teacher must also be alert to the fact that a learned emotion can generalize to other similar stimuli. Emotional upsets interfere with learning efficiency. Affective factors as well as cognitive factors must be taken into account in the classroom. A warm accepting teacher can do much to alleviate anxiety in the students, and to enhance the motivation of learning activities.

SUMMARY

A brief overview of factors affecting the development of personality was given. These included heredity, maturation, primary and secondary needs, cultural influences, and emotional development.

The goal of educational psychology is to identify major causes of behavior. Some basic laws of motivation as they relate to the personality of the individual are discussed in Chapter 3.

THE DEVELOPMENT OF PERSONALITY
STUDENT OBJECTIVES

In an objective type test which may include matching, multiple choice, and one word answer questions, the student will be able to:

(K) 1. List the two major components of personality.

(An) 2. Choose whether given characteristics are due to environmental, hereditary influences, or a combination of both.

(K) 3. Recognize physiological traits when given a series of descriptions.

(S) 4. Explain how gratification or frustration of primary needs affect the acquisition of secondary needs.

(An) 5. Identify unlabeled theory statements with respect to which one of the three views of personality they pertain to.
(An) 6. Discriminate between primary and secondary needs.
(K) 7. List three factors which correlate with specific family child training practices.
(K) 8. Describe the responsibility generally attributed to the school in child development.
(K) 9. List a reason for a student performing at a lower intellectual level than he is capable of as mentioned in the text.
(K) 10. Describe a failure commonly demonstrated by middle-class teachers toward lower-class students.
(An) 11. Contrast the effects of a traditional family background influence to a family where individual development is emphasized.
(S) 12. Devise a teacher approach for each of the two major techniques used to modify an emotional behavior.
(K) 13. Identify two major classifications of factors which must be dealt with in the classroom.
(E) 14. Evaluate critically an article on personality development.

Chapter 4
MOTIVATION

Generally, theory precedes the development of scientific achievements. For instance, in physics the theory of relativity gave rise to the use of atomic power as a source of energy, and in psychology Freud's theory of personality and behavior aided the development of the treatment of neurotic symptoms. These achievements have led educational psychologists to look for basic laws of learning and motivation before suggesting specific procedures which might enhance performance in the classroom. The aim of educational psychology has been to identify, with some precision, the causes of behavior. Certainly educational psychologists have been more concerned with the "how" of behavior than with the "what."

Motivation is defined as providing motive to an individual. It means to incite, impel, or stimulate the active interest of a human being through an appeal to associated interest or by special devices. For instance, the act of motivating a child to learn new words is achieved by making the study interesting or appealing.

Motive is understood as an unknown quantity within a person such as a need, idea, organic state or emotion that incites him to action. It is also the consideration influencing a choice prompting an action. A prompting force or excitement working on a person to influence volition or action may help to amplify the definition of motive. Motive, when used in music and art, implies that there is a controlling idea or force which caused the artist to paint a picture or, as in the case of a musical composition, a musical phrase that is reproduced and carried throughout the score of a musical composition. The motif of a work of art may be interpreted as giving insight to why the artist created the piece.

Motivation is usually understood in terms of internal (intrinsic) and external (extrinsic) forces. That is to say, that the motive may come from within a person or from without. Extrinsic comes from the Latin word *extrim* (the outside) and the Latin word *secus* (to follow). Extrinsic is defined as lying outside and not forming a part of the entity or belonging properly to the entity. It means that the motive is not contained in or does not occur within the individual. External or extrinsic forces come solely from the outside and are extraneous. Extraneous applies to what is exterior or unrelated but may be interjected with or interpreted as a part of the consideration. Intrinsic means belonging to the inner most constitution or essential nature of a thing and is not merely apparent, relative, or accidental. Intrinsic means originating and included wholly within the entity. For instance, one could observe that a child loves to read and therefore he reads intrinsically. On the other hand, if the teacher said to the student: "Read five pages and I'll give you candy," this would be extrinsic motivation.

PSYCHOLOGICAL CONCEPTS OF MOTIVATION

The Encyclopedia of Educational Research lists four theoretical positions which have developed to explain the instigation, direction, magnitude, and persistence of human behavior. These four theories—associative theory, drive theory, cognitive theory, and psychoanalytic theory—were developed early in the history of psychology. The associative theory, probably the oldest principle of causation, states that if one event frequently follows another event, then it is logical to assume this to be principle. Kurt Lewin described this as the principle of adhesion. Before the 1920s instinct was among the most frequently mentioned causes of behavior, but the concept of instinct declined during the 1920s and was replaced by the concept of drive (Woodworth, 1918). Although pure associative theory and the drive-times-habit approach provide a mechanical framework of human behavior, more cognitively oriented psychologists have maintained that behavior is purposive—i.e., guided by an anticipated goal. The psychoanalytic theory is frequently regarded as the psychological theory of motivation. The broad scope of this theory is too complex to explore in this book, but selected principles of the theory can be discussed here. These are (a) anxiety and fear, (b) achievement, (c) anger, (d) affiliation, (e) creativity, (f) curiosity, (g) imitation, (h) modeling, and (i) self-concept which is an integral factor of each of the previously listed tenets. Current trends suggest a growing realization that behavior is complex and determined by many factors; no single concept, such as instinct, need, or association, can fully explain the different patterns of behavior. Organisms are viewed as being constantly active and striving. The focal point is on the direction of behavior rather than on its instigation.

Anxiety and Fear

Anxiety and fear as conditioned stimuli were explored in detail by Neal Miller (1959), a student of Hull. He placed a rat in a black box for several weeks. The rat was fed and made comfortable. After the rat had become familiar with the comfortable life in the black box, Miller placed the rat in a white box and administered a severe electrical shock. Miller noticed that the rat (a) attempted to escape even before the shock was administered, and (b) learned new habits that would enable escape from the white box when earlier learned escape routes were unavailable. The implications of this effort suggest that fear is a secondary or acquired drive, that fear functioned similarly to drive even though it was not inherent, but was learned. Conditions for the acquisition of fear were demonstrated experimentally. Hull's theoretical system has been challenged by educational psychologists as being inadequate. Clearly, anxiety and frustration develop for many other reasons other than biological survival, although survival is one of the underlying causes. One teacher who realized fear was ruining her life made a worry table. In totaling her table she discovered:

40%—will never happen; anxiety is the result of a tired mind.
30%—about old decisions which I cannot alter.
12%—others' criticism of me, most untrue, made by people who feel inferior.
10%—about my health, which gets worse as I worry.
8%—"legitimate," since life has some real problems to meet.

Current research focuses on effects of failure on anxiety (Finch, 1975), phases in coping as it relates to anxiety (Falek and Britton, 1974), and classroom anxiety and the examination performance of test anxious students (Osterhouse, 1975). Finch (1975) attempted to determine the sensitivity of the State-Trait Anxiety Inventory for Children (STAIC) to changes in anxiety in emotionally disturbed children. Thirty-six children (mean age, 11.24 years) in residential treatment were administered the STAIC. (Separate assignments were given for males and females to ensure equal and random distribution to each group.) These groups included a failure group, a failure plus ego-involving instructions group, or a test-retest group. The group receiving failure plus ego-involving instructions reported the greatest anxiety increase for both A-State and A-Trait portions or the STAIC. Results are given on the basis of the state-trait anxiety theory and as indicative of the vulnerability of A-Trait anxiety to stress seen in emotionally disturbed children.

Falek and Britton (1974) surveyed literature on psychological responses to terminal illness, bereavement, physical trauma, and environmental trauma, noting common findings of four coping patterns: denial, anxiety, anger, and depression. These are viewed as attempts to return to psychological homeostasis. Denial involves no initiation of behavioral change; the anxiety phase reflects cognitive reception of the situation and intellectual activity directed toward regaining equilibrium. Anger results when these efforts fail, and the ensuing frustration leads to depression. This represents an emotional awareness and a combination of emotional and cognitive efforts to regain a psychological steady-state. It is suggested that these patterns are important considerations as the teacher plans individualized instruction.

Osterhouse (1975) examined the academic performance of a total of 412 low, moderate, and high test anxiety university students (as measured by the Inventory of Test Anxiety). These two classrooms differed significantly in the mean level of anxiety aroused by examinations. When differences in classroom anxiety were not a consideration, significant negative linear trend was observed between anxiety level and academic performance. No differences were found in the academic performance of low test anxiety within the two classrooms. However, a significant interaction was observed between classroom anxiety level and the academic performance of moderate and high test anxiety. Moderate test anxiety obtained slightly higher examination scores in the High Anxiety section than in the Low Anxiety section, while the opposite was true for high test anxiety.

The results of current research suggest that the important motivating component of many drives is actually a learned tendency and is not acquired. Humans learn to be discontented or anxious in the absence of these goal objects. For example, there may be stimulus signals signifying a lack of effect. This learned anxiety cue then functions to energize the appropriate behavior to reach such a goal. The current successful studies of fear and anxiety as acquired drives are making it possible to test the theory more effectively on humans. The reason for this is that once anxiety and/or fear is established as a drive, then one could differentiate people as to the degree to which they were chronically highly anxious or chronically low in anxiety.

Achievement

Achievement motivation appears to be linked to the kinds of groups in which the student works. Different levels of achievement motivation may arise as a function of the environment. The Hawthorne studies (Roethlisberger and Dickson, 1939) illustrated the influence on behavior of social, interpersonal influences, democratic styles, and peer expectances on performance. Research suggests that people are influenced by other people in terms of level of aspiration and behavior participated in. Asch (1956) discovered that a significant number of individuals publicly stated that a physically shorter line was longer than one that was in fact physically longer. These statements were made, for the most part, when the individual was confronted by the unanimous, though wrong, opinions of others. Data seem to suggest that individuals achieve best when the group influencing that behavior is one in which individuals are highly attracted to each other.

Parental influence, however, is not always effective. "You ought to be ashamed," the father told his loafing son. "When George Washington was your age, he had become a surveyor, and was hard at work." "And when he was your age," the boy replied, "he was President of the United States."

The literature search reveals studies on task-goal attributes (Steers, 1975), achievement, motivation and self-esteem (Husaini, 1974), and relationships of fear-of-failure and need achievement motivation to a confirming-interval measure of aspirational levels (Teevan, 1975). Steers (1975) analyzed the relationship between employees' task goals and supervisory performance as moderated by achievement among 133 female 40-44 year old first-level supervisors working under a formalized goal-setting program. It is concluded that individual difference factors, like achievement, must be considered in any comprehensive theory of goal setting.

Husaini (1974) examined the relationship between achievement motivation and self-esteem of 115 American and 67 East Indian male college students by administering the Thematic Apperception Test, the Rosenberg Self-esteem Scale, and an actual/ideal self-rating. Results suggest the influence of cultural variability upon the lack of achievement and self-esteem relationship of the two cultures.

Teevan (1975) found that studies have shown that individuals characterized as motivated by a fear of failure tend to set levels of aspiration defensively.

Anger

Anger may be related to fear but the basic drive is entirely different. Anger is a strong feeling of displeasure and unusual antagonism. It is rage, fury, indignation, or wrath. Motivation caused by anger may be instantaneous or planned. Planned action against a force may manifest itself in the form of a vendetta. Basically, fear is fundamentally a preparation for flight while anger is a preparation for fighting. Anger is usually a response to frustration, a conflict between two opposing tendencies. One response tendency in frustration is the original tendency which evoked the situation, the other is an alternative response aroused by the frustrating or interfering conditions themselves.

There are advantages and hazards involved in anger. Anger provides extra energy and may frighten someone else into doing what a person wants him/her to do. When an angry person vents his anger on another, it provides him with a feeling of well being. While venting anger, however, the individual may lose respect. Unfortunately, the anger vented may be misspent energy and leave the person with feelings of guilt. An angry reaction often disregards the rules of society or a group. More importantly, the angry person is reacting emotionally rather than responding intellectually. Anger may take another route. The angry person may react by regressing to an earlier behavior.

There are several ways to avoid anger. Anger, a response to frustration, may be controlled by the problem-solving approach. For instance, Jane was responsible for keeping the bathroom clean. Regrettably, her brother John seemed always to leave it looking like a deserted battleground.

Jane's job was to keep the room clean, not to pick up after her brother. She turned her anger into action. She made a point of making use of the room before her brother and leaving it in a worse state of disarray. It was not long before John received the message loud and clear.

Other ways of dealing with anger include a change in a point of view and thus eliminating the stimulus to anger. Even though a person changes his point of view completely, however, he will never be able to avoid the stimulus to anger completely. Then how does one deal with anger? One way may be similar to the suburban husband who was about to leave his home for the city when his wife detained him.

"John," she said, "I wish you'd go out to the kitchen and give Bridget a good talking to before you go to work."

"How's that?" he asked, "I thought you were satisfied with her."

"So I am, dear," replied his wife; "but she's beating some carpets for me this morning, and she does it better when she's angry."

Anger is a usual but unfortunate response to frustration. It is unfortunate because it neither alleviates the frustration nor improves the situation. A review of the literature reflects studies conducted on aggression and heat (Baron and Bell, 1975), reflections on narcissism and narcissistic anger (Kohut, 1973), and on effective assertive behavior (Hewes, 1975). Baron and Bell (1975) conducted a study in which 64 male undergraduates participated in an experiment designed to examine the effects of level of prior anger arousal, exposure to an aggressive mode, and ambient temperature on physical aggression. On the basis of A. Bandura's (1973) social learning theory of aggression, they predicted that uncomfortably hot environmental conditions would be most effective in facilitating later aggression when subjects had witnessed the actions of the model and had been exposed to strong provocation from the victim. They predicted that it would be least effective in this regard when they had neither witnessed the actions of the model nor been exposed to prior instigation. Results indicated that high encompassing temperatures facilitated aggression by nonangered subjects but actually inhibited such behavior by those who had previously been provoked.

Kohut (1973) outlines various types of narcissistic expression, distinguishing between narcissism as a general category and narcissistic anger as a special category. In modern man, Kohut wrote, narcissistic (self-admiration) needs conflict with the western world value systems of social obligation. The degree of ego autonomy and ego dominance is a consideration in his study. This leads to the concept that narcissism finds different forms of expression according to ego positions. The genetic and dynamic influences of narcissistic and object-directed motivations are compared, and the phases of ego development are described in detail along classic psychoanalytic lines. Kohut believes that a recognition of this factor will aid the teacher in understanding motivation from this aspect.

Hewes (1975) identifies two kinds of assertive responses that can be identified when anger has been aroused. Humanists separate expressions of anger from verbalized angry attacks. The latter usually elicit counterattack, whereas the expression of anger is inclined to produce a change in effect, or some verbalized self-observation, or a defensive position.

Affiliation

The intrigue of why we choose those people with whom we associate has drawn the curiosity of marketing agencies and educational psychologists for many years. The influence of the choices has a great impact on the economy. Affiliation is defined then as the bonding or attachment to another human being, material object, or esthetic value. Harvey Cox in *Seduction of the Spirit* discusses how advertisement agencies influence the affiliation of the American people by appealing to their moral and spiritual values as well as their sexual fantasies.

The gamut of our emotional life may orbit around affiliation choices. The happiness or unhappiness of a marriage will affect most of one's relationships and activities. Simultaneously, choice of friends, activities, home, neighbors, and occupation will determine the economic level of one's life. The notion of affiliation as applied to the classroom has caused educators to focus on individualized instruction; consequently, instruction is ap-

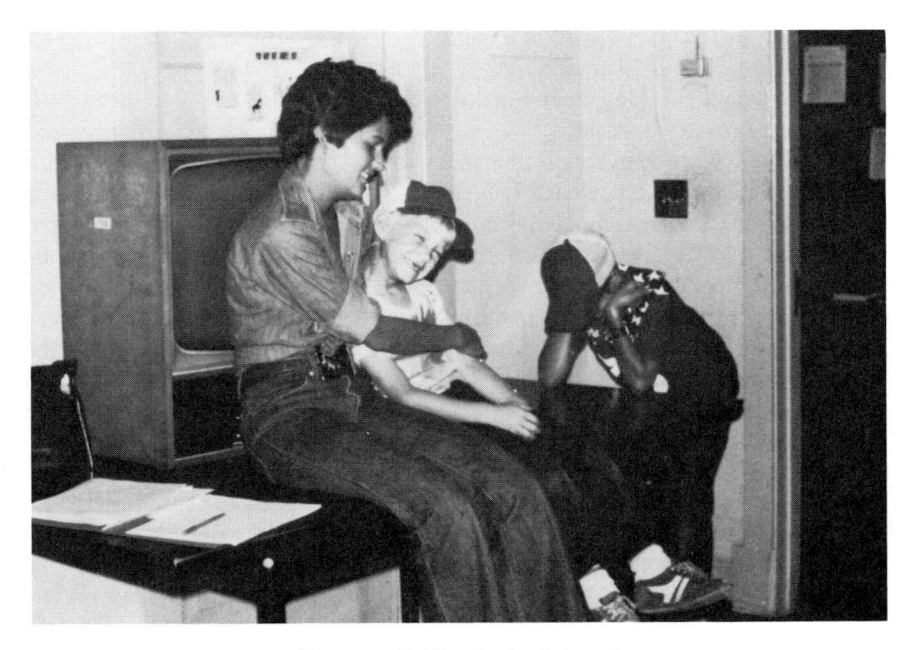

Group activities foster interest.

proached now on the basis of cooperative learning tasks, not on the basis of fierce competition.

This shift in pedagogical practice is based on the need for association. This need is seen as the desire to be associated with another person or persons, whether for cooperative effort, companionship, love, or sexual satisfaction. The tenets related to the need for affiliation are generalizations stating how the functional relationships between precepts and ideas are established and revealed. Originally there were four such laws: the Law of Similarity, of Difference (or Contrast), of Succession, and of Coexistence. These were eventually summarized and expressed in the Law of Contiguity.

The manifestation of affiliation is conceptualized in an individual or individuals as their need to draw near and enjoyably cooperate with one another, to form friendships and remain loyal, to please and win the affection of important individuals. This is also called affiliative need fulfillment. Association is then a functional connection between psychological phenomena established through experience or learning whereby the occurrence of one tends to summon the other. It can also be defined as a bond between ideas.

Successful companionship requires a commitment of loyalty and devotion from those in an affiliative association. The classroom teacher must match carefully those individuals placed in cooperative learning situations. For instance, a Scotsman was overheard in a conversation concerning his friend.

"I hear yer frien' Tamson's married again."

"Aye, so he is. He's been a dear frien' to me. He's cost me three wedding presents an' two wreaths."

A survey of current research efforts in the area of affiliation produces a revealing study on TAT need achievement and need affiliation in minimally brain-injured and normal children and their parents (Touliatos and Lindholm, 1975). This study contrasts the need for achievement and the need for affiliation in the families of 16 minimally brain-injured children with that in 16 families of normal children. The families in this study were matched on age, sex, and birth order of the children and on education of the fathers. Needs were measured with Thematic Apperception Test (TAT) cards. Minimally brain-injured children and their mothers were lower in achievement motivation than the normal children and their mothers. Results indicated that fathers were in the same direction, although not significant. Parents of minimally brain-injured children appeared to have a different pattern of influence on their offspring than parents of normal children. The achievement needs of the mothers in the former group were positively related to their children's behavior. The achievement needs of the fathers in the latter group were negatively related to their children's behavior. There were no differences in motivation related to affiliation.

Creativity

Creativity is a rather elusive talent, but much effort has been directed recently toward developing tests that measure creativity. These tests have to measure the number, variety, or novelty of ideas that are evoked or summoned by a given problem or task. The creative student is in effect a diversified thinker. Divergent thinking, as compared with convergent thinking, is more flexible and fluid. It is not confined to the information at hand but it permits a deeper and richer flow of ideas. To cope with problems confronting an uneasy nuclear-age world it is necessary to go beyond the obvious, time-worn and dated methods of problem solution.

Creativity is divided into the following aspects: product, process, personality and environment. Environment includes not only external forces, but those forces that work from inside the individual. Environment, as related to creativity, includes the mood of the individual as well as environmental conditions such as the temperature, humidity, etc. Creativity means to bring into existence, to produce original solutions, or unconventional alternatives.

A process of creativity explored in more recent years is brainstorming. This is a process by which a small group of individuals are brought together and presented a problem. In this group, alternative solutions are proposed by various group members. Utilized in the business world more than by the classroom teacher, brainstorming is essentially a creative activity.

Research currently under study centers upon creativity and ego development (Workman and Stillion, 1975), teaching reading through creative movement (Humphrey, 1974), and behavior in microdrama situations and measures of creativity (Ekstrand, 1975). Workman and Stillion (1975) gave 58 female undergraduates the Torrance Tests of Creative Thinking (TCT), Figural form B, and the Washington Sentence Completion Test to investigate the hypothesis of a positive relationship between creativity and ego development. A Spearman rank-order correlation coefficient was calculated for ego development at the .01 level. Originality was correlated at the .05 level. Results are discussed in terms of A. Maslow's (1968) theories concerning highly developed persons, and potential preconscious aspects of the creative process. An exploration of this research effort may provide the teacher clues to understanding creativity.

Humphrey (1975) describes a procedure for working through creative movement to develop comprehension first in listening and then in reading. The technique used by Humphrey involves a learning sequence of auditory input to movement to auditory-visual input.

Ekstrand (1975) studied the relationship of observable creative behavior in microdrama situations to a number of test measures of creativity. Student teachers were evaluated by three raters in drama situations and given five creativity personality tests. Correlations between ratings and tests were generally low but positive. A trend to higher correlations was demonstrated when original and "irrelevant" test responses were analyzed separately. Subjects with high ratings tended to have individualistic traits according to the personality instrument.

Curiosity

Curiosity is defined as the desire to know. Unfortunately, parents have treated this psychological aspect as an undesirable tendency. When little hands have gone exploring, parents often scold and punish the small child's exploratory efforts. Then curiosity becomes "something that kills the cat" and something that provokes the wrath of parents upon "the backside." Similarly, other groups in leadership positions have labeled curiosity a blamable trait. For instance, when the early Christian Church controlled large numbers of individuals, the Church disallowed certain information and discredited secular information. Selection and censorship of library materials often becomes a matter of controversy because only one side of an issue is presented and curiosity is discouraged among students.

Administrators, teachers and parents are often frightened by the unfamiliar. This fear is reinforced by the framework of one's coping patterns which are built around certain familiar patterns of living, habits, and value systems. Curiosity, a close ally of creativity, often brings new coping patterns, new patterns of living, different habits and new value systems.

A teacher tells a story about his father which describes best why he always seemed to be better informed about more things than almost anyone else.

"Uncle George," he said one day, "why are you brighter than the rest of the family?"

"I'm not," his father replied. "I just have more curiosity." Analogously, the requirements placed upon teachers, administrators, and parents by our modern technological and scientific society are new and can only be met with new and different solutions to complex problems. In effect, curiosity and creativity must become an integral part of the psychological credo and practice.

Identification and Imitation

Identification is the practice of feeling that a person is in the role of someone else. For instance, when one views a film or a television program the actors draw the viewer into the plot and there is a feeling of close identity with one of the characters in the play or film. A viewer may support a boxer or sports figure. A boy may imagine himself as a hero, and a girl may place herself in the role of the heroine. A person who spends a great deal of time before the television set may be participating in drama to escape from his/her own difficulties. The individual may become a hero, a lover, or a person of wealth and distinction while viewing television, but in real life may be struggling to get along and may be depressed by troubles and problems.

Everyday millions of students watch television programs at home and identify with certain characters in programs they view. They identify with these fictional characters, and escape temporarily from the problems of their own family life and school life. Identification can also occur when one reads stories, novels, biographies or autobiographies. One lives the part of one of the characters and may in real life, consciously or unconsciously take on some of the other person's characteristics.

The teacher may take advantage of this phenomenon to motivate students to explore various facets of learning. For instance, suppose the teacher has the task of teaching students to understand how the United States was launched as a nation and at the same time look at the leaders of this early revolutionary movement. By involving the students in a film about George Washington in which he is shown realistically involved in a plot, students may be drawn into the film and emotionally identify with the character. This teaching strategy lends itself to further exploration of the

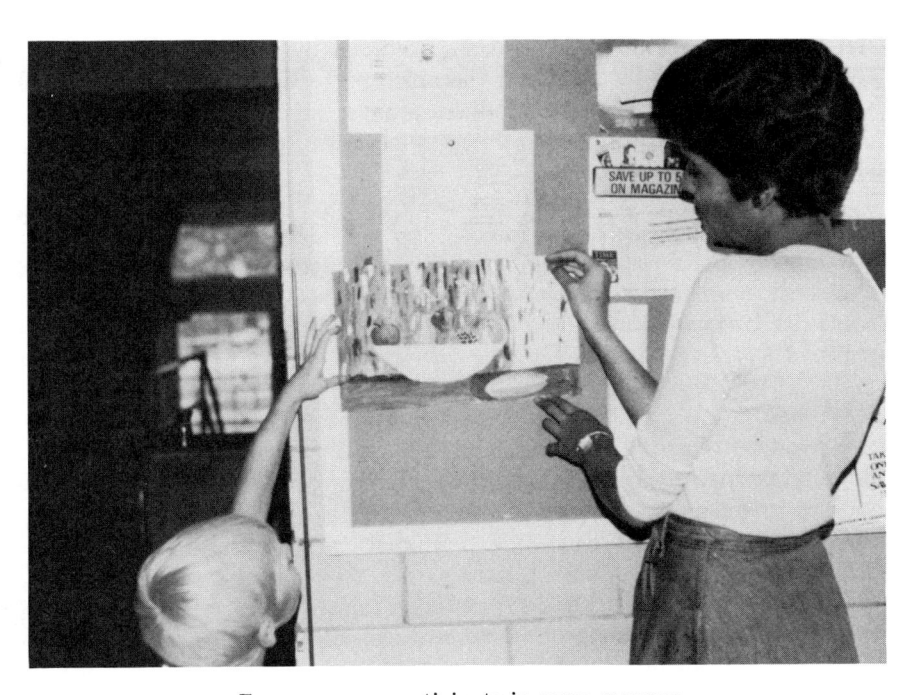

Everyone can participate in some manner.

period. When contrasted with the traditional method of "open your textbook and read from pages 112 to 220 about "The American Revolution," it becomes apparent that the first method is more desirable.

Not only can the teachers utilize this strategy for teaching but can help students choose identity roles that are appropriate to their culture and society. A mistaken or inappropriately assumed identity role may bring unhappiness to the student as he attempts unrealistic goals or pursuits.

"As I was going over the bridge the other day," said an Irishman, "I met Pat Kelly." "Hewins," say I, "how are you?"

"Pretty well, thank you, Connelly," says he.

"Connelly," says I "that's not my name."

"Faith, then, no more is mine Kelly."

"So with that we looked at each other again, an sure enough it was nayther of us."

A survey of current research in the area of identification indicates such representative studies as identification and imitation in the treatment of juvenile offenders (Fleischer, 1975), the role of imitative social learning in identification processes (Meissner, 1974). Fleischer argues that no therapeutic change can occur unless there is some degree of identification between patient and therapist. Three effects of imitation on the therapeutic process are described and conditions which foster the identification and imitation are explained. Other issues considered include therapist warmth, therapist activity, the myth of therapist perfection, and the ethics of therapist modeling. If research indicates that a therapist-patient dialogue is essential to identification, then the more complex student-teacher relationship is even more crucial.

Meissner (1975) discusses the respective contributions of social learning phenomena to the process of introjection and identification, emphasizing the imitative behavioral learning processes because they are the best studied and most clearly articulated of social learning theories. Learning and identification processes interact, influence each other, and appear to be integrated.

Modeling

Models as used in industry and education have been defined traditionally as specimens or cross sectioned parts. Models are working prototypes of an apparatus or a machine. Models and modeling serve very practical functions. Much of the U.S. space program, for instance, has depended heavily upon lunar related models to train astronauts. Similarly, the behavior of the astronauts had to be related to certain scientific information relative to weightlessness and restrictive activities as applied to certain utilitarian physiological functions. Recently, however, the use of models and modeling has become a widespread practice among professional educators.

Models and modeling can be deceptive and hazardous. They can overemphasize a symbol, overemphasize form, oversimplify, and can cause, in some instances, a blindness to the real presentation. Although most behavior patterns can be considered models, nothing by itself is a model. Models are presented to enable students to think about the world experienced.

Studies under the subject of modeling investigate the effects of watching the behavior of others on one's own behavior. Basically, this research has centered around the conditions under which models and modeling may be used as a mechanism for changing the behavior of the observer. For example, data from the literature indicate that the aggression in others that leads to some reward or the cessation of some punishment is more likely to be repeated by the observer than is the behavior that is punished. If we presuppose that people learn about attainable values through observation, then this type of finding certainly fits in with the general conclusion that aggression is more likely to be participated in if there is some type of value to be obtained. Research data reveal that aggressive behavior as a response to frustration is inhibited when punishment for such behavior is anticipated. Hostile behavior is inhibited by a high degree of anticipated punishment. High status people are usually less likely to be the objects of aggression than low status people. The groups and individuals who are usually chosen as scapegoats and as targets for aggression are generally weaker individuals. The likelihood of revolution resulting from frustration is more likely to occur after a period of rising expectations.

Translated to the classroom it becomes obvious that teachers need to be alert to this information because it relates directly to social interaction among students. The responsibility of the teacher is then viewed in terms of protecting the low-socioeconomic against the hostile actions of the higher-status student. Simultaneously, the students need to help the victim to learn protective measures. Some representative research efforts recently conducted reflect on an overview of recent research in depression (Akiskal and McKinney, 1975), and the stereotype approach to the modeling and simulation of an elementary school (Windeknecht and D'Angelo, 1975).

Akiskal and McKinney (1975) wrote that disciplinary fragmentation and semantic controversies have obscured the impressive advances made in the area of depressive disorders during the past decade. They translate data derived from psychodynamic, sociobehavioral, and neurobiologic research into a clinically meaningful framework. Ten models of depression are reviewed with a special focus on newer models supported by empirical and experimental studies. A new model is proposed which incorporates and synthesizes findings from selected schools. Depressive illness is conceptualized as the feedback interaction of three sets of variables at chemical, experimental, and behavioral levels, with the diencephalon serving as the field of action.

Windeknecht and D'Angelo (1975) describe an approach to the modeling and simulation of evolving societies of individuals. This idea is based on the notion that a society of interacting stereotypes retains important properties of behaviors of real societies of individuals. These can be made to interact with other individuals. A model of an hypothetical six grade elementary school is sketched, and a digital computer simulation of the model is described to test the feasibility of the stereotype approach.

Self-concept

It is most unfortunate if, in growing up, a person develops a highly distorted, faulty, or otherwise unrealistic picture of himself, whether that picture is too flattering or too belittling. How he sees himself will determine what he does with himself and how he feels about himself.

An unfavorable self-concept brings uncomfortable feelings with respect to the self. This may occur directly from one or several experiences and, unfortunately, may stay with us for a long, long time. Thus, if a boy's older brother is always humiliating him by making fun of his ability, his appearance, or his social activities, the boy will have uncomfortable feelings with respect to himself and his acceptability, and these feelings may persist and become a part of him. When our self-concept includes such unrealistic ideas as "I am not acceptable," "I am not a likable person," "I am not the equal of those with whom I would like to associate," when we customarily feel anxious and uncomfortable in the presence of others, we are said to have inferiority feelings, often referred to as an inferiority complex. There are instances in which the person is not acceptable, and then his feelings of inferiority are justified. But often the self-concept is inadequate, distorted, or even false, and then the individual may suffer from uncomfortable and emotionally disabling feelings which are not justified.

Betty is a very attractive high school girl. She is healthy, has an attractive face, and an alert mind. She is courteous and pleasant in her relationships with people. Since she is careful about her appearance, she makes a good impression on people when she first meets them. Yet Betty is troubled by feelings of inferiority. It is difficult to believe that a person who is so obviously superior should have such a feeling; yet she does. Why do such persons feel inferior? The answer is this: At some time in their childhood or youth something occurred to give them the idea that they were inferior and to produce uncomfortable feelings in connection with their peers. These feelings have remained with them as they developed. As a result, even though their common sense may tell them that they are as good as others in appearance, intelligence, and likability, they still feel inferior.

What sorts of experiences build such feelings into the personality? Anything that sets a person apart from his peers in some unfavorable manner may give him inferiority feelings, though certainly it need not have done so. Some sources of inferiority feelings are physical characteristics, socioeconomic factors, sensitivity to criticism, sensitivity to slight, dislike for advice, hunger for praise, and failure.

People with inferiority feelings may strive too hard to impress others with their worth. They may stay away from those with whom they feel inferior and uncomfortable, and may seek to behave so as to lessen their discomfort. Symptoms of inferiority feelings include a lack of social ease and constant unfavorable criticism of others. Closely related to self-concept is the theory of self-actualization. This approach is known by such names as self-actualization theory, humanistic psychology, third-world psychology, and so forth. It is a highly important movement among many psychologists interested in such problems as personal and social growth, institutional and organizational change and development (see Chapter 3).

Self-actualization theory has some of its philosophical ground in the work of the existentialist philosophers. Basically, the self-actualization theorist argues that the individual has been prevented from engaging and behaving in a meaningful, self-actualizing manner by the conditions and environments in which he is not able to fulfill himself (or self-actualize). The role of the educational psychologist is to identify the factors and conditions that are preventing the person from reaching his self-actualizing state and then to work toward eliminating these restricting forces so that one can move toward self-actualization.

A number of motivational theories of this type have been suggested, but the one which has served as the base for the self-actualization movement is the one by Maslow (1954, 1968).

Maslow's Proposed Behavioral Differences Between Deficiency-oriented and Growth-oriented Individuals (Korman, 1974)

The person who is deficiency oriented is the person whose basic needs have not as yet been satisfied and who is oriented toward achieving these satisfactions. His behavioral characteristics are likely to be the following:

1. Rejecting of one's own impulses.
2. Satisfying a need or achieving gratification leads to tension reduction.

The person who is growth oriented is the person whose basic needs have been satisfied and who is motivated toward self-actualization. His behavioral characteristics are likely to be the following:

1. Accepting of one's own impulses.
2. Satisfying a need or achieving gratification leads to excitement, growth, and change.

3. Gratifications achieved are relatively short, stable, and temporary in nature.
4. The goals sought are species-wide in nature.
5. Behavior is dependent on environmental cues.
6. Others are viewed primarily in terms of their ability to satisfy one's own basic needs.
7. Tends to be ego-centered, concerned with self, and the satisfaction of basic needs.

3. Gratifications achieved tend to change the person in a relatively permanent way.
4. The goals sought are individualistic, unique to the individual.
5. Behavior is relatively independent of environmental cues.
6. Others are viewed objectively for what they are, rather than in terms of their ability to satisfy one's own basic needs.
7. Tends to be ego-transcendent, not as concerned with the self as with the nature of the world.

Representative research efforts focus on the effect of teachers' inferred self-concept upon student achievement (Aspy and Buhler, 1975) and adjustment differences between junior high school students (Busselen and Busselen, 1973). Aspy and Buhler (1975) investigated the relationship between teachers' level of Inferred Self-concept (ISC) and the cognitive growth of their students. One hundred and twenty third graders were matched according to sex and I.Q., and their cognitive growth was determined by pretesting and posttesting with the Word Meaning, Paragraph Meaning, Spelling, Word Study Skills, and Language subtests of the Stanford Achievement Test. The six teachers' levels of ISC were calculated by three raters who completed Parker's Self-concept Checklist after observing each teacher for one hour. Results show that the levels of SC were related positively to the subjects' cognitive growth at the .01 level of significance for four of the five subtests and the total gain.

Busselen and Busselen (1973) studied the influence that family relationships, peer groups, and society have on the formation of the individual's self-concept. An investigation of the effects of success and failure modifying effects on the ability to estimate the area of 20 geometric figures is presented in this study. Two groups of 98 third year high school students were individually tested. One group received three pretask successful trials and the second group received three pretask failure trials. The results of estimates of performance, before and after pretask trials, demonstrated that previous success positively affected perception of performance while previous failure had a negative effect. Furthermore, males were more affected by success and females were more affected by failure.

The one concept which plays a major role in the individual's life and is directly affected by each of the motivational aspects previously discussed is one's self-concept. Through experimentation, individuals gain an image of themselves through the actions and reactions of others. Ideally one would have a clearly defined picture of his physique and personality. In reality, however, mirror images are deceptive and full of error.

EXTRINSIC MOTIVATION

Extrinsic motivation may take the form of reward, punishment, or social motivation. The desirability of reward (positive) over punishment (negative) as a motivational device is a dominant consideration today in educational psychology. The individual is recognized as having internal needs that are best met through positive reinforcement. The need for success and self-actualization are certainly important aspects of today's society. For instance, in studies such as *Comparison of Self-motivated Air Force Enlistees with Draft Motivated Enlistees* by Lonnie Valentine and Bart Vitola (1970), it became evident that the performance of those individuals who are members of an organization or group because they "have been self-motivated" is superior to those who have been forced to join. In fact, Congress recently voted for an all volunteer army over an army supplied by the Selective Service Act. In the classroom negative reinforcement may be expressed by the teacher who tells his student: "you'll get a lick with the paddle for each spelling word you miss." Another student is told by his teacher: "you will be given extra recreational time for each word you spell correctly on the quiz." Although positive reinforcements or rewards are not always possible or practical, they are to be preferred.

Social motivation is viewed as (a) peer group motivation, (b) student teacher personality interaction, and (c) family motivation. The need for peer acceptance seems to reach a zenith at puberty. It is at this point in development that students become extremely sensitive to the actions and reactions of peers. Students constantly monitor these reactions for clues to their own identity and mold their self-image accordingly. The child who has for a number of years depended upon his parents for approval, acceptance, and support now looks to his peers for acceptance. As a result of the need for social acceptance and image-building, the individual has a tendency to conform. Gradually, students conform to some of the written and unwritten laws of society. As the student conforms in the educational and social process, he tends to feel more uncomfortable each time he fails to do so. Coupled with the fact that the mores and values of society to a large degree are shaped by those in the society who have a vested interest, the student soon learns that his very economic survival depends to a degree upon accepting what those in the power structure dictate. Student conformity is reinforced by the need for security, for a sense of worth, and for good relationships with others. Even those young groups in the society who support a revolutionary approach to dress appear to conform to the uniform of their group. Data seem to indicate that human beings not only have a need for biological reproduction but they also possess the need for intellectual reproduction. Those students, for instance, who are most like the teacher may be the ones who receive the most rewards, regardless of the quality of academic performance.

In summary, extrinsic motivation may come to humans in the form of reward or punishment. Social motives come through the various social interactions of the student with his peer group, his family, and teachers. The family and teachers may influence the individual to a greater degree in the prepubescent period while peers exert more influence from adolescence through adulthood. The need for social contact and the high degree of influence exerted by social extrinsic motivation may be attributed to the fact that humans continually dtvelop their self-image by monitoring the actions and reactions of those around them.

INTRINSIC MOTIVATION

Intrinsic motivation may be viewed as humanistic and cognitive. While Clark Hull was developing his theoretical system at Yale University, Tolman at the University of California at Berkeley was developing an alternative approach to motivational phenomena. Tolman's approach to motivational phenomena conceptualized behavior as being caused by various internal and external environmental stimuli and by disequilibrium situations. Environmental stimuli and human characteristics, such as age, previous training, heredity, and specific physical characteristics, result in three primary intervening variables. These variables are (a) demands for specific goals, (b) the degree to which the goal is available, and (c) the person's expectancies of achieving the goal in the specific environment in which he finds himself. Tolman's model of the cognitive approach to motivation is as on page 57 (Korman, 1974).

The humanistic approach is exemplified by Abraham Maslow (1964). He has theorized that human need structures are organized in a hierarchical system and that needs lower in the hierarchy must be fulfilled before higher order needs in the hierarchy.

There are seven needs identified in his system. These are as follows:

1. Physiological needs are the needs of the individual for food, water, oxygen, sleep, activity and sensory satisfaction.
2. Safety needs are seen as degrees of anxiety concerning threats to the body and security.

3. Belongingness and love needs are expressed in a hunger for affectionate relationship with others. This need implies the giving and receiving of love.
4. Esteem needs are reflected in the desire for self-respect, status, recognition and confidence.
5. Self-actualization is explained as "what a person can be and what he must be."
6. The need to know and understand is a desire which permeates all other needs.
7. The aesthetic need is conceptualized as the need to see beauty in one's surroundings rather than that which is ugly.

Observable Antecendent	Intervening Variables	Observable Sequences
Environmental Stimulation	Goal Demand	Direction of Behavior
Physiological Stimuli	Goal Expectancy	Behavior Persistence
Previous Learning	Goal Availability	Toward Specific Goal
Influence of Heredity		
Maturity		

Maslow states that there are certain preconditions necessary for the gratification of basic needs. These preconditions are not ends in themselves, but are close to these basic needs. These preconditions are:

1. freedom to speak and do what one wants without hurting others,
2. freedom to investigate and seek information,
3. freedom to express one's self, and
4. freedom to defend one's self with honesty and justice.

In his hierarchy of needs, Maslow states that as a lower need is fulfilled another need emerges. However, there are exceptions. For instance, one act may satisfy more than one need, i.e., the giving of food not only satisfies the physiological but the safety and perhaps the love needs of the individual.

Maslow believes that human beings from different cultures share a common bond. People differ in superficial areas like clothing, types of food and housing. However, the basic needs are the same. Even in primitive societies people wished to be loved and to be safe.

PRACTICAL CLASSROOM APPLICATIONS OF PSYCHOLOGICAL CONCEPTS

Application	Concepts
Gain Student Attention	Curiosity and Anxiety
Students are Aware of Expectations (Student Related Objectives)	Achievement
Success—Each Student Should Attain Success Daily	Achievement
Feedback is Crucial in Maintaining Motivation	Creativity and Curiosity
Practical Application of Academics, Especially Disadvantaged	Identification-Modeling Affiliation Creativity
Utilization of Intrinsic and Extrinsic Motivations (selected)	Anxiety Achievement Anger Affiliation Creativity Curiosity Identification Modeling Self-concept
Anxiety—Motivator not Inhibitor (Testing Situation)	Anxiety
Competition and/or Cooperation	Affiliation Anger Achievement Modeling
Group Work	Affiliation
Praise and/or Nonpraise	Modeling Anxiety Achievement
Child's Interest	Affiliation Imitation Modeling
Enthusiasm	Modeling Identification
Exhibit an Active Interest in Student	Affiliation

Needs can change our perception of the environment and, therefore, become motivators. As motivators they are not to be viewed in the context of stimuli and response because all basic needs are motivators of behavior. Extrinsic motivation viewed from the aspect of need satisfaction is at the reflex level.

Gratification of needs plays an important role in this theory. If an important basic need is frustrated in its attempt for gratification the person may become ill. When normal growth occurs in the absence of frustration, the individual develops into a self-actualizing human. It is worth noting here that when an individual historically has had his needs met fully, he may go for extended periods of time with ungratified needs without adverse effects to his mental and emotional well-being.

According to Maslow, first the physiological needs such as hunger and thirst must be fulfilled. When this has taken place, the security needs become relevant as determinants of behavior. This in turn is followed by social needs, self-esteem needs, and finally the self-actualization needs. Some believe there is not adequate evidence of the validity and adequacy of this theory. However, there is evidence for the theory in the works of a large number of writers who have proposed that if we decrease hierarchy, external control, and specialization, and if we allow people to control their own destinies more, we will get a great degree of what Maslow and others have called self-actualizing behavior.

SUMMARY

Motivation means to incite, impel, or stimulate the active interest of an individual. Historically four theories explain the instigation, direction, magnitude and persistence of human behavior. Psychological and scientific discoveries quickly outdated these simple theories. Psychologists now view motivation as a complex phenomenon viewed from several psychological tenets. This chapter discussed nine of these: anxiety, achievement, anger, affiliation, creativity, curiosity, identification, modeling, and self-concept. Extrinsic and intrinsic motivation were discussed as they applied to the classroom teacher. Practical applications of the nine psychological tenets of motivation are presented.

Chapter 5 is basically concerned with learning and its application to the classroom. Both associative and cognitive theories are discussed.

MOTIVATION
STUDENT OBJECTIVES

In an objective type test which may include matching, multiple choice, and one word answers, the student will be able to:

- (C) 1. List and explain (with his/her own examples) all methods of practically applying psychological concepts.
- (C) 2. List and explain Maslow's Hierarchy of Needs System.
- (C) 3. Give examples of Extrinsic and Intrinsic motivators.
- (An) 4. Discriminate among Psychological Concepts of Motivation.
- (K) 5. Match selected researchers with Psychological concepts of motivation.
- (An) 6. Distinguish between Humanistic and Behavioral concepts of motivation.
- (App) 7. Apply Humanistic and Behavioral concepts to given situations.
- (S) 8. Analyze given situations and apply corrective procedures.
- (K) 9. Define the following terms: (a) Motivation, (b) Motive, (c) Extrinsic, (d) Intrinsic.
- (S) 10. Categorize examples of motivators into the categories, Intrinsic or Extrinsic.
- (E) 11. Explain in given situations why the given practical application of Psychological Concepts was effective and/or ineffective.
- (K) 12. Define the theoretical concepts of motivation.
- (C) 13. Explain how Social Motives affect classroom motivation and learning.
- (A) 14. Identify how the theoretical Psychological Concepts of otivation affect the student's self-concept.
- (S) 15. List three of his/her own reasons as to the applicability of the results of the study they reviewed.
- (E) 16. Critically review a research article on motivation and explain it to the class (summarize).

Chapter 5
LEARNING

Learning is fundamental to every form of psychological theory. This chapter will point out that although there is little disagreement among psychologists as to the significance of learning and the pervasiveness of learning in nearly all forms of human activity, there is a marked difference in the ways learning is perceived.

Kimble (1961) wrote that the roads to defining learning are two-fold—the factual and the theoretical. Factual definitions relate learning to observable events in the physical world; theoretical definitions are concerned with descriptions of basic processes that the learning theorist believes to be prerequisites for learning to occur. Hebb (1966) related the theoretical definition when he discussed central nervous system (CNS) activities, the neural messages that occur in the CNS roadways. "Learning means a change in the direction of message in the CNS." In discussing response probability as a basic principle in the learning process, Skinner (1953) offered the reader a factual definition: "We may define learning as a change in the probability of response, but we must also specify the conditions under which it comes about." Hebb was describing changes in the CNS that may be difficult to observe; Skinner was concentrating on the frequency and altered probability of an exact observable response under explicit observable conditions.

There seems to be a general concensus among psychologists and educators that learning is a comparatively stable change in behavior that results from practice or a change in one's environment or experiences with learning representing an intervening process or variable. Fatigue, maturation and drugs are not considered as changes caused by experience or change in one's environment. The central question has been one of differentiating learning and performance. Learning is implied from observed performance.

Learning cannot be measured directly. It can only be inferred from the observed behavior. Therefore, we can only measure performance, not learning. Mistakenly, teachers conclude that students have learned if they answer questions correctly. However, this may or may not be true. Failure to provide a correct answer does not always indicate that learning has not occurred. It is impossible to elicit student responses reflecting all learning. Relevant cues may not be present. Teacher constructed tests frequently do not consider motivation, maturation, and evaluation, nor, are they conclusive.

Kimble (1961) perceived learning as a change in behavior potentiality. The human organism may acquire capabilities to perform some act through learning, but the act itself may not occur. He wrote that learning "refers to long-term changes of the organism produced by practice . . . (while) performance . . . refers to the translation of learning into behavior." Learning then is defined as a change in behavior potential caused by reinforced practice. Reinforcement, expressed in this manner, becomes an example of the empirical law of effect that is basic to current learning theory. Thorndike (1931) stated this law as "acts followed by a state of affairs which the individual does not avoid, and which he often tries to preserve or attain, are selected and fixated, while acts followed by states of affairs which the individual avoids or attempts to change are eliminated."

He modified the law in 1932 by indicating that rewarded responses were always strengthed but that punished responses did not always diminish in strength, thus leading to an emphasis on reward as a primary determiner of behavior.

Contemporary views of learning consider the learner's past experiences, his present abilities, his needs, and his feelings. The learner undergoes some kind of experience; he does not simply learn by aging. His experience includes perception, manipulation of ideas, feeling and general motor activity. Consequently, learning may be construed as changing one's potential for seeing, thinking, feeling, participating through experiences which are partially perceptual, intellectual, emotional, and psychomotor. This is based on the assumption that it involves processes in the nervous system that to this point have only been partially identified. Psychologists' inability to identify the exact processes involved in learning accounts for the many learning theories in educational psychology.

The processes by which learning occurs are then the subject of scientific investigation, and it is to be expected that the study of learning will provide knowledge that educators can use in designing instructional environments and in carrying out the educational process. The purpose of scientific investigation is to understand, predict and control behavior so that students can come closer to attaining their potential. Controlled behavior represents the psychological approach to learning, and the attainment of a student's potential represents the practical approach.

Research into learning processes encompasses five areas. The first function, is exploratory research, which scientists call theoretical or basic research, is described by questioning attitudes and the relative independence of the application or further development of existing knowledge and processes. Fundamental development is the second research principle. This is the investigation of the many variables relevant to principles discovered in exploratory investigation. The third function is specific development. This area relates to the fact that after the theory of specific learning is established the various artifacts involved in the process must be produced. Design and proving is the fourth function. Finally, training and follow-through is required.

TYPES OF LEARNING

In studying the processes of learning, the researcher should distinguish four types of learning: respondent or classical conditioning, operant reinforcement conditioning, imitation or modeling learning, and cognitive learning. The first three of these types are included in the broad category of associative learning theories known as S-R (Stimulus-Response) theories.

Respondent or Classical Conditioning

Ivan Pavlov, the Russian physiologist, was the pioneer of research in respondent conditioning. He observed in his work with gastric secretions in dogs that stimuli that were often present at the time the dogs were offered food came to evoke salivation in the animals even in the absence of food. For instance, the footsteps of the experimenter as he came into the room often evoked salivation in dogs. This occurred even though the dogs were unable to see or smell food. Pavlov assumed that the stimulus of the footsteps came to be affiliated with food. His research focused on the analysis of this event, which he labeled the conditioned reflex, meaning that a reflex would occur in the presence of conditions. In a typical experiment, a stimulus that prior to training had no ability to evoke a particular type of response becomes able to do so in the experiment. Under normal circumstances, a bell sounded near an animal will usually evoke no more than a startled response. Likewise, under normal circumstances, a dog would be expected to salivate when food is present.

Pavlov's conditioned reflex experiment was a training experience in which the previously neutral stimulus of a bell was made by pairing it with food to induce the response of salivation, which it normally would not do. Bell sounds preceded the display of food. The animal salivates at the sight of the food. Ultimately the dog paired the bell and food. Because the food produces salivation, it is referred to as the unconditioned stimulus (UCS); the salivation to the food was identified as unconditioned response (UCR); the learned response of salivation at the sound of the bell was called the conditioned response (CR).

Pavlov's works are characterized by five principles. These are as follows:

1. Orienting response is a very complex response involving neural, sensory, circulatory and motor reactions. Orienting response was first noted by Russian psychologists when a conditioned stimulus was presented but prior to the presentation of the unconditioned stimulus. For example, the dog

would perk up when the conditioned stimulus was presented (but prior to the presentation of the unconditioned stimulus). The dog would look for the sound and be tense and alert. The physiological reactions were described as cessation of the alpha rhythm of the brain, more blood rushed to the head, the pupils dilated, respiration stopped momentarily, and muscle tonus increased. In 1960 E.N. Sokolov reported that if the previously mentioned physiological changes were not extreme, they enhanced the learning process. However, if the conditions were extreme or went unnoticed the animal did not learn.

2. Extinction is the time when the conditioned stimulus does not evoke the conditioned response. Pavlov's experiment involved ringing a bell (conditioned stimulus) in the presence of a dog and then presenting food (unconditioned stimulus) to the animal so that the dog associated the two as one. Eventually, the bell would sound and the animal would salivate without the food being present. To continue the association of the bell and food in the mind of the dog, food must occasionally be presented. However, if food is withdrawn and the bell continues to sound, the association is weakened and no longer evokes salivation (conditioned response). When this occurs extinction has taken place.

3. Spontaneous recovery may occur after extinction following a lull. It should be noted that the response is not as strong as the original. There appears to be a gradual fading of the conditioned response if the unconditioned stimulus is not presented, until the conditioned response is not observable.

4. Stimulus generalization means that a similar stimulus may evoke the original response. The greater the deviation from the original stimulus the lesser the response in the individual.

5. Stimulus discrimination is a term usually used in relation to stimulus generalization to mean that an individual will not respond to similar stimuli but only to the original stimulus.

Current research and work in the field of conditioning is concerned with the establishment and strengthening of stimulus-response relationships. Classical conditioning has dealt primarily with reflex-type responses where an already strong response is brought under the control of a stimulus other than the original stimulus. An exchange of stimulus control occurs from the original unconditioned stimulus to the new, or conditioned stimulus (Grant, 1964). In instrumental or operant conditioning, the distinction between response learning and bringing the response under the control of an appropriate stimulus can be brought into focus.

Operant Reinforcement Conditioning

The term "operant" refers to a class of responses that are "emitted" by the organism rather than forced out of the organism or "evoked" by some known stimulus as Pavlov's views might suggest. The term "operant responses" is also referred to by such terms as "voluntary" as contrasted with involuntary behavior. Reflex responses are elicted, as in classical conditioning, and are identified as respondents. Proponents of analysis of behavior based on operant conditioning techniques and reinforcement theorists form a group of behaviorists who tend largely to minimize theoretical considerations and focus on analyzing the functional relationships among events. Behaviorists believe that behavior is changed because of the individual's interactions with the environment.

For example, instead of dealing with the repression of unacceptable thoughts, as psychoanalysts do, the behaviorist Burrhus F. Skinner suggested that it is more important to circumvent the inner causes and to emphasize the questions that ask "why the response was emitted, why it was punished, and what current variables are active." Skinner in his first book, *The Behavior of Organisms,* identified two types of conditioning which he called type S and type R. Type S conditioning is defined by Skinner as the operation of the simultaneous presentation of the reinforcing stimulus and another stimulus. In type R conditioning the reinforcing stimulus is dependent upon a response. This distinction between classical (respondent, involuntary, type S) and instrumental (operant, voluntary, type R) conditioning is not completely accepted by many learning theorists because the criteria are ambiguous.

Skinner has continued the work in learning research pioneered in America by Edward L. Thorndike, who worked throughout his career to discover laws of learning patterned after the laws of physics. Thorndike and his followers were largely responsible for three important themes that have dominated learning theory in America: associations between stimuli and responses, objective observation of overt behavior, and the establishment of laws of learning. Skinner developed his systematic views in the 1930s and has exhibited overtones of empiricism or a practical orientation. The important concern to Skinner is how behavior can be modified. He has been especially identified with the reward psychology advocated by Thorndike.

In his Harvard laboratory, Skinner conducted experiments in modifying behavior which have been very influential. His experiments were arranged so that an animal would perform a task and then receive a reward, or "reinforcer." In one experiment, rats were required to depress a lever to obtain food in the form of one pellet at a time. In another, a pigeon was required to peck at a small target in order to receive food. Skinner was able to study the conditions under which the rate of bar-pressing or target-pecking could be changed at will by the experimenter.

His emphasis upon emitted responses does not mean that Skinner is unconcerned with the influence of stimuli. He considers stimuli as the environment in which behavior occurs rather than viewing stimuli as instigators of behavior. In one experiment, a rat is rewarded for pressing a bar in the light and not rewarded for pressing it in the dark. Consequently, the rat learns to press more actively in the light. Skinner does not consider the light as a causative stimulus, but as a "discriminative stimulus" (SD).

It should be noted here that two very important phenomena in stimulus control are generalization and discrimination. These are processes delineating the characteristics of a response as it becomes related to a stimulus. Generalization refers to the characteristic of behavior that occurs when an individual learns to act in a certain way in the presence of a distinct stimulus. This behavior also occurs when stimuli having common properties with the stimulus or stimulus class used during the original learning is present. Discrimination learning is a term applied to the process by which stimuli came to acquire selective regulation over behavior (Kimble, 1961).

When a learner has acquired a response to a particular stimulus, it is obvious that other like stimuli will also elicit the response that has been learned; once a response has been reinforced in one situation, the probability that the response will occur in other like situations is increased significantly. Early in its development the concept of stimulus generalization was associated with neural mechanisms (Pavlov, 1927). Hall, Spence, and Skinner considered it as an empirical behavioral phenomenon and deemphasized neural claims. They departed from the traditional Pavlovian experiments in this research.

Discrimination learning is a process by which stimuli come to acquire selective control over behavior; particular situations set the occasion for the manifestation of behavior in that situation. It is understood that a student has learned to discriminate between stimuli when he responds differentially and reliably in various stimulus situations. The concept of reinforcement in learning has had wide acceptance and has had a great influence on educational psychology. This concept translated into educational principle would read as follows: When a student's responses result in need reduction symbolized by reward, approval, or praise, the responses or activities perceived by the pupil as having led to these pleasurable consequences are strengthened.

Recently a southern high school was having difficulty in handling study halls. A baseball was rolled down one aisle of seats. This brought laughter. The teacher responded by going to the back of the room and threatening to "beat the hell out of the person that rolled the ball." This was but one in a series of such incidents, all of which elicited the same fighting responses from the teacher. What the teacher did not recognize was that each event was a reinforcement for the very kind of behavior he was attempting to stop.

POSITIVE REINFORCEMENT, NEGATIVE REINFORCEMENT, PUNISHMENT, AND THEIR CONSEQUENCES

Behavior may be controlled by positive reinforcement, negative reinforcement and punishment. Each of these may be identified as separate entities.

Positive reinforcement produces favorable consequences to the individual. This increases the chance of the behavior occurring again.

Negative reinforcement involves the withdrawing of an aversive stimulus (some sort of punishment) thereby increasing the probability the response will occur again. For example, a bully has applied pain to the student. The student agrees to an act and the pressure of the twisted arm is relieved.

Punishment is often confused with negative reinforcement. It involves the presentation of an aversive stimulus (some sort of punishment) or the withholding of a positive stimulus thereby decreasing the probability of response reoccurrence. For instance, when a child misbehaves, he is immediately spanked. Or, a privilege may be withdrawn to punish the child.

Punishment may lower the frequency of undesirable behavior but it may also produce undesirable side-effects. For example, negative emotions may be aroused or be conditioned to the content material or the teacher. The use of punishment or negative reinforcement bring two different types of behavior. These are escape and avoidance behavior. In escape behavior the individual learns to respond to eliminate aversive stimuli. In avoidance behavior the student may learn to avoid the painful experience (stimulus) by responding before the aversive stimulus is presented.

According to Skinner, there are decided three disadvantages in the use of punishment to control behavior. These are:

1. Behavior is temporarily suppressed.
2. Negative emotional responses are aroused which can interfere with learning.
3. Intense anxiety is created forcing students to avoid school, teacher, and parents.

However, this may be considered a positive reinforcer for some. Skinner and other behaviorists advocate the use of positive reinforcement at all times in order to change behavior. One means of accomplishing this in the classroom is by use of the Premack Principle. This principle uses high probability behavior to reinforce low probability behavior. For example, after the child completes an assignment he is allowed free reading time. The assignment is viewed as the low probability behavior and the free reading time as high probability behavior.

Schedules of Reinforcement

Skinner has demonstrated four schedules of reinforcement. These are ratio (fixed and variable) and interval (fixed and variable). Ratio refers to amount. There is a gradual reduction of reinforcement to a gradual increase in performance. A fixed ratio indicates an established procedure for a reinforcer. For instance, ten responses may require five reinforcements. A variable ratio means that this ratio fluctuates. For example, five responses may require 3 reinforcers, or 2 reinforcers, as 5:3 or 5:2.

Interval refers to time. The reinforcement is delayed on a time schedule relative to a prior reinforcement; for instance, a five second delay before the presentation of a second reinforcer. When a schedule is present the interval is fixed. But when intervals depend on the decision of the rewarder as he observes behavior the intervals are said to be variable.

Analogies to ratio and intervals may be seen in industry. Industry uses two methods of paying its workers. One is known as "piece work" or paying an employee on the basis of production. This is similar to ratio because behavior is reinforced on the number of responses or production.

Secondly, workers are paid by salary. This is similar to interval because behavior is reinforced on the basis of time rather than production. The disadvantage here is that the individual decreases his response rate after reinforcement and then gradually increases as the time of reinforcement approaches.

Two other factors affecting learning are: variable schedules tend to result in more persistent behavior and extinction is delayed longer with variable patterns than with fixed patterns.

Fixed ratios offer an advantage in shaping behavior. In fixed ratios there is one reinforcement to one response. Once the behavior has been established the fixed ratio may be changed to a variable schedule of reinforcement.

Knowledge of these learning concepts can be applied to the classroom by:

1. Associating content to be learned with a pleasant experience, such as a smile.
2. Use positive reinforcers in the classroom instead of negative reinforcers or punishment.
3. The teacher should be aware of what constitutes a reinforcer for each student.
4. Intermittent reinforcement is generally more effective in retention of material learned than continuous reinforcement.

5. The social learning history of the student will provide the teacher a better understanding of the child's problems.
6. Through the use of rewards the teacher can shape desirable classroom behavior and eliminate undesirable behavior in a similar manner.

Model Learning

Clark Hull, a leader in the area of applying S-R theories to social behavior, experimented with rats with an idea of developing a general theory of human behavior. Subsequently, Albert Bandura and Richard H. Walters chronicled in *Adolescent Agression* (1959) a study in which social learning principles were used to analyze personality development in a group of middle class delinquent boys. In 1963, the two authors presented their theory in *Social Learning and Personality Development.* Bandura and Walters focused on imitation and reinforcement patterns as they influence socially acceptable and socially unacceptable behavior. They accentuated the ways in which self-control is developed and maintained through self-rewarding and self-punitive responses. They stressed that an understanding of the learning of self-control is necessary to any theory of personality development.

Imitation or modeling plays an important role in developing behavior patterns. New responses are learned through observation. For imitation to occur there must first be identification. Individuals do not imitate those with whom they do not identify. Recently a psychologist from Florida observed at a resort beach in that state that teenagers who had come for the Spring vacation were spending more of their time observing each other than their idol. Students seemed to be learning desired behavior by observing each other. Some psychologists believe that many of the very important learnings, particularly those related to emotional expression and social interaction come about largely through modeling behavior after that of another person. For example, a fearful mother may easily transmit fear to a child without directly teaching fear. A small boy who admires his father may pick up the mannerisms of his father.

It has been observed that a model is most influential as an eliciting stimulus when the behavior that is imitated is likely to be rewarded. Albert Bandura reported this in *Nebraska Symposium on Motivation,* a study of imitative responses made by children in various social-role contexts. In one study, experimental social groups of a man, woman and child were formed. In each group, one adult was either the controller of rewards, the recipient of rewards from the other adult (consumer), or was ignored. Observations revealed that the children modeled their behavior after the adult who controlled the rewards. It was the one with power that exerted the most influence in the social group. It was also discovered that characteristics of the observer determined to some degree the nature of imitative responses. Some persons are more susceptible to imitative behavior than others.

There is presently a controversy over the extent to which media affects the individual. There appears to be a correlation between media exposure and aggression. If, as Bandura and Walters hypothesize, that modeling occurs in childhood, then the question arises as to whether or not modeling occurs in adults. For example, if a child watched television early in his life, will he tend to be more aggressive in adulthood?

In 1972, a longitudinal study (10 years) concerning this question was conducted by Eron, Huesmann, Lefkowitz and Walder. The results of this study indicated:

1. The sex of the child significantly affected the learning and display of aggression. (Boys were more aggressive than girls.)
2. Exposure to aggression during childhood may initiate aggressive behavior at a later time due to vicarious or direct reinforcement.

The U.S. Surgeon General's Scientific Advisory Committee on Television and Social Behavior conducted a similar study in 1972. This study indicated that for some children, particularly those with a predisposition to aggressiveness, viewing aggressive behavior and aggressive behavior itself were causally related for short periods of time.

They also concluded that the time period ranged from minutes to hours with the possibility of being causally related for longer periods of time (days to years).

The classroom implications of these results are:

1. The teacher should be an appropriate model for culturally acceptable behavior.
2. The teacher should be aware that as a model they are influencing student behavior.
3. Educators should teach children culturally acceptable methods of venting hostile feelings.

Cognitive Learning

The learning of complex problems must include considerations such as meaningfulness, organization, and understanding. Investigation in this area involves the study of relationships and how people learn to see relationships among a variety of experience items.

This phenomenon was first widely publicized by the German psychologist Wolfgang Kohler in the *Mentality of Apes* (1925). Kohler emerged as the leading spokesman for a group of German psychologists who began experimenting with chimpanzees at about the same time that Thorndike was expanding and revising his laws. They asserted that man and higher-order primates learn through the development of insight. They described their belief in the importance of patterns with the word "Gestalt" ("configuration").

Kohler's best known laboratory work involved a chimpanzee named Sultan. Sultan learned to use short sticks to rake objects toward him when he was feeling lazy. On one occasion, Kohler arranged a banana and a very long stick outside Sultan's cage so that the stick was nearer the cage than the banana, with both objects out of reach. Sultan attempted repeatedly to reach the banana with short sticks, but to no avail. After a period of brooding, he noticed the short stick, long stick and banana. He used the short to obtain the long stick and then used the long stick to reach the banana.

Kohler believed that this experience exhibited a rearrangement of Sultan's thought pattern, a new application of prior knowledge.

An essential ingredient of cognitive learning theory was demonstrated in this experiment—the perception of new relationships, or insight. Sultan's preconditioning did not solve the problem; it was insight into the relationship between the sticks and the banana that brought the solution. Cognitive learning theorists do note, however, that Sultan's prior experiences with the basic ingredients in the problem were necessary before insight could take place. Other apes who had not had any prior raking experience failed to solve the problem.

Kohler's work stimulated other Gestalt psychologists to develop theories stressing the importance of insight. Among these psychologists are Jerome Bruner, Arthur Combs, Donald Snygg and Kurt Lewin. The work of Lewin has been very important in the application of Gestalt psychology to cognitive learning theory (cognitive-field theory).

One of Lewin's most significant contributions to cognitive learning theory has been his concept of life space. The life space of a person is the sum total of information the observer needs to know about that person to understand his behavior in a specific psychological environment at a specific time. It is important to note that this concept illustrates an essential difference between the S-R associationists and the cognitive-field theorists. The cognitive theorist believes that to understand behavior one must consider how persons seem to themselves, not just how they seem to others.

Learning may be analyzed as association, perception, reinforcement, cognitive organization, imitation, and neural action. Four types of learning were explored here. These were respondent, operant, modeling and cognitive learning. Various learning theorists have contributed to our understanding of behavior by focusing on one or the other of the aspects of learning. For instance, the Gestalt psychologists assign perception a major role in the study and explanation of learning.

Classroom application of these principles involves the following:
1. There should be an increase in the quality and quantity of the child's academic experiences.
2. The student should be allowed freedom of thought so he can manipulate and synthesize concepts and experiences without fear of criticism (brain storming).
3. The individual should learn from his mistakes.

RETENTION

One of the persistent allegations of the critics of education has been the large masses of today's graduates who are deficient in the simple fundamentals. For instance, businessmen often complain that recent graduates cannot spell or use simple punctuation. A common explanation for young graduates' lack of skill in English is attributed to forgetting.

The study of forgetting has been the subject of research for some time in the field of educational psychology. Unfortunately, many of these studies have involved material learned by rote-memory (often nonsense material) which one would expect not to be representative of certain disciplinary skills. A typical laboratory experiment to measure retention involves subjects who are asked to master certain learning tasks. The task(s) may be motor or verbal or both. At a point following the learning session, the experimenter measures the amount of learned material that the subjects have retained. The interval period may vary from days to months.

There are at least six reasons why an individual forgets learned material. These are disuse, interference, repression, motivation, reorganization, missing stimuli or factors. Disuse offers a logical "common-sense" reason for forgetting. Many skills learned in school may have no utilitarian value for the learner. Consequently, he never uses them or for that matter ever thinks about them. This competition among ideas may account for some ideas dominating the thoughts of an individual while others seem to be buried.

Much of the research conducted today reveals that forgetting is caused by interference from other experiences and from competing learning. Interference between old and new learning may work in either of two directions or both. Interference is either retroactive or proactive. Retroactive interference is defined as new learning impeding or blocking old learning. Proactive interference is old learning blocking new learning. If recall failure is present, it may be due to (retroactive) interference of new learning; but, new learning does not mean there is a failure to recall.

	Proactive Interference		
	Learn	Learn	Test
Experimental	A	B	B
Control Group	Rest	B	B

	Retroactive Interference		
	Learn	Learn	Test
Experimental	A	B	A
Control Group	A	Rest	A

Figure 1. A means of determining the presence of Proactive or Retroactive Interferences is illustrated above.

By teaching a control group and an experimental group, content A and content B, the experimenter is able to determine either proactive or retroactive interference.

Research on interference (McGeogh 1940-1941) has demonstrated that interference in learning increases as the number of competing associations increase; interference is greater the more similar the material in two learned tasks. Moreover, the more incomplete the learning, the more it becomes vulnerable to interference.

Another reason for forgetting is repression, based upon a Freudian principle. This theory states that material which is unpleasant and anxiety-producing to the learner may be forced below the conscious level. Although most educational psychologists do not consider it a major cause of forgetting, clinical and research data does support the concept as one effective cause of forgetting.

Motivation refers to the student's intention to learn. If a student wants to learn the material it is highly probable he will retain the content. This means the teacher must establish the motivation for learning.

Missing stimuli or "Q" factors are those cues necessary for a particular response. When these are not present, the particular response will not occur. For example, an ambiguous test question may be too general to evoke a response.

Reorganization is an imperfect, defective, or faulty recollection of prior learning. It is theorized that individuals never forget what is learned. Memory, many psychologists believe, functions very similarly to a computer retrieval system. The problem lies in gaining access to the information. The memory retrieval system is often faulty in that bits of information from various storage areas are reorganized in an inaccurate manner. Humans often remember only portions of the material and fill in the missing blanks with what they think may be the answer. Or, they may combine two facts like the wrong date and with the correct event.

Out of this survey of retention, the important factor for the teacher remains that of teaching for good retention. This may be accomplished by fostering efficient techniques of learning, being confident the material has meaning, building intent to remember, teaching beyond initial mastery, and providing review.

This may be accomplished by efficient techniques of retention such as:
1. Overlearning of material,
2. Review frequently,
3. Emphasize meaning and structure,
4. Distributed practice or small portions of learning over a long period of time,
5. Whole-part method or teaching various components and bringing the total picture into focus,
6. Cognitive dissonance (Zigarnec, 1927) or tendency to remember unfinished tasks better than finished tasks,
7. Discovery method (especially effective with intelligent highly motivated students when no clearly defined solution is present,)
8. Sense of accomplishment (works well with slow learners),
9. Questions should be related to the method of presentation,
10. Students should be taught under a variety of conditions so learning can be applied under varying life experiences,
11. Individuals should learn from their mistakes through discussion of errors,
12. Play the "devil's advocate" by changing sides in the discussion.

TRANSFER

The goal of teaching is to produce desirable changes in behavior that will carry over into new situations. For instance, teachers intend training in English composition to produce good writing. In fact, there can be little justification of education if what is learned does not transfer. However, all learning cannot be evaluated on the basis of transfer. Transfer of learning is said to occur when previously learned material has an influence on the learning or performance of new reponses. Theoretically, anything that is learned can be transferred. A simple example of transfer is as follows:

A student learns . . . . 2 X 3 = 6
This should aid him in learning that . . . . 3 X 2 = 6
and . . . . 30 X 20 = 600

There are four theories of transfer: formal discipline, identical elements, generalization and transposition. Formal discipline theory of transfer is based on the assumption that the mind is similar to a muscle. A muscle can be built through exercise, such as running, swimming, etc. Analogously, this theory suggests that the mind can be built through mental exercise in mathematics, Latin, geometry and other fields of rigorous mental activity.

The identical elements theory, proposed by Thorndike in 1913, explains transfer in terms of identical elements. Transfer occurs when two tasks have like elements. For instance, students learn to add because this task is very similar to counting. By identifying identical elements in tasks, learning may be facilitated. For example, when the common words of Spanish and Portuguese are learned the foreign language student has learned parts of two languages. All that remains to be learned are the exceptions.

The theory of generalization is on outgrowth of the identical elements theory. This theory states that similar stimuli evoke the same response. For example, a dog that responds to middle C will also respond to middle D, or, a child who has been taught that a four legged creature is a cat will call all four legged animals cats until corrected.

Transposition is defined as the transfer of general principles from one area to another. For example, a monkey is presented two plates. One is four inches in diameter and one is six inches in diameter. He is taught the reward is under the four inch plate. The four and six inch plates are exchanged for six and eight inch plates. Which will he choose to receive his reward? If he learned his lesson, he will choose the six inch plate. The principle involved is that the reward is under the smaller plate.

Transfer may also be negative. Negative transfer occurs when one stimulus requires two responses. The effect of negative transfer may be reduced or eliminated by:

1. Reducing reactive inhibition (allowing the student to return to the problem at a later time if no solution is forthcoming).
2. Reducing the content to smaller units and teaching the smaller units.
3. Brain storming.

These principles are suggested for effective teaching for transfer:

1. Formulating clear cut objectives.
2. Drawing upon those items in the course content which are applicable to life.
3. Selecting instructional materials which make relationships clear.
4. Fostering learning with a variety of examples.
5. Providing practice in transfer (never assume transfer).

SUMMARY

In the application of laboratory procedures derived from learning research, the behavior theories have fallen heir to the very problems that plague the research scientists. Foremost among these is the problem of definition; the precise definition of such basic concepts as stimulus, response, and reinforcement remains a theoretical and experimental problem. The precision with which experimental contingencies can be stated in both the laboratory and the clinic is a continuing philosophical, theoretical and research issue. In this chapter it has been demonstrated that learning has many facets. This creates a complex situation for the classroom teacher who may be unfamiliar with the psychological ramifications of learning. Learning was defined and four types of learning were examined. Causes of forgetting were examined and suggestions were given the teacher candidate for effective teaching.

The teacher bears the primary responsibility for maintaining order and dealing with misbehavior in the classroom. Discipline problems, solutions to misbehavior, and conditions conducive to learning are explored in Chapter 6.

LEARNING
STUDENT OBJECTIVES

In an objective type test which may include matching, multiple choice, and one word answers, the student will be able to:

(K) 1. Define the following terms: (a) Learning, (b) Classical Conditioning, (c) Operant Conditioning, (d) Reinforcement, (e) Negative Transfer, (f) Elicit and Evoke, (g) Emit, (h) Contingency, (i) Transfer.
(An) 2. Distinguish between the four types of Learning.
(C) 3. Give examples for each of the four types of Learning.
(K) 4. Name a proponent for each of the four types of Learning.
(K) 5. State the results of research conducted in each of the four types of Learning.
(An) 6. Identify and give illustrations of principles effecting Learning.
(E) 7. Determine the type of Learning used in situational questions on a test.

- (S) 8. Formulate a method for overcoming factors effecting learning in a given situation.
- (C) 9. List all methods of enhancing retention and learning.
- (A) 10. Apply in a given situation one or more methods effecting learning and retention.
- (C) 11. List and give examples of the four different theories of transfer.
- (C) 12. List and give examples of methods for enhancing transfer.
- (A) 13. Indicate a process for neutralizing negative transfer.
- (An) 14. Analyze a situation and apply the method of enhancing transfer most appropriate to the situation.
- (An) 15. Distinguish between Retro and Proactive Inhibition.
- (C) 16. Analyze the four types of learning and give the advantages and disadvantages.
- (C) 17. Give examples for four out of six causes for forgetting.

Chapter 6
DISCIPLINE

The orderly functioning of any social system requires some regulation of its members. This is also true of a school system. If the system is to operate properly, the conduct of pupils must conform to conditions that are conducive to learning. Indeed, principals and teachers are by statutes and board regulations charged with the responsibility of maintaining order in the school. This reponsibility may be extended to the pupils coming to and from school. The primary responsibility of maintaining order and dealing with the various forms of disorder falls upon the shoulders of classroom teachers.

These procedures by which order is maintained in a school are referred to as discipline. Generally the system of discipline in a school will reflect the system found in the broader society. In the Western world the system of discipline characterizing society has been moving from force to persuasion and then to self-control. Teachers resort to force only after self-control and persuasion fail.

Under the older form of school discipline, order was maintained by rules and regulations enforced by penalties. The severity of the punishment varied with the kind and degree of the infraction. Among the penalties frequently employed were reprimands, detention, withdrawal of privileges, corporal punishment, and expulsion; however, these methods have been used less frequently in recent years. The trend today is to seek proper conduct through learning rather than by authority. The pupil is guided in the development of self-control and responsibility to other pupils and the school. This view of discipline entails the organization and operation of the school in such a way that situations leading to disorder will largely be avoided, and at the same time the maximum opportunity for the development of self-control is provided. Opportunities are created for pupils to participate in school management and in selected types of classroom situations whereby a sense of responsibility for proper behavior is developed. According to Morse and Wingo, students should be given only the freedom they can responsibly handle.

Although the dynamics of human behavior are not completely understood, it is certain that all behavior, whether normal or abnormal, is the product of a highly complex interaction involving biological, psychological, and environmental factors. Thus, the physiology of the individual's brain, his developmental history, store of cognitive information, interpersonal relations, sensory input, and affective experience, as well as the characteristics of the environment with which he interacts are included among the variables which determine an individual's behavior and personality.

The manipulation of these various variables or determinants can result in significant changes in behavior. Some of these behavioral factors are manipulated more easily than others. For instance, relatively little can be done to change certain types of permanent brain damage, or the pathological elements in a student's early social and familial experiences. On the other hand, other variables that determine behavior can be changed.

Traditionally, discipline has been considered as a means of learning. A quiet, orderly classroom has been an important objective of teachers and principals, who have believed that this is the situation most conducive to learning. A classroom characterized by "pin-drop quiet" was considered the mark of a good teacher, and teachers were hired and fired largely on the basis of their ability as "disciplinarians." In teacher-training institutions, courses in "classroom management" taught the tricks of the trade in achieving a quiet and orderly classroom. Supervisors rated teachers largely on their ability to "maintain control."

One can see clearly the relationship of this concept of discipline to the educational philosophy which has prevailed in the public schools during most of the years since their origin. It can be pointed out that schools have been predominantly insitutions in which teachers have tried to force children to achieve goals adults think they should achieve. Adults established a curriculum of subjects which they deemed important, and then demanded that children learn it. Knowledgeable educators questioned this practice and have come to realize that in all too many respects there is little relationship between the learnings required and the daily life and purposes of the children. This is especially true of children from slum neighborhoods who hold a fiercely pragmatic view of schooling. This is also true for girls, while among boys such behavior as inattention and class disturbance is the most frequently occurring form of misconduct. A study comprising 225 high school principals revealed that they rated the following as the most serious forms of misbehavior: lying, showing disrespect for faculty, petty thievery, and congregating in the halls and lavatories (Henning, 1949).

The perception of teachers regarding the seriousness of various types of misbehavior appears to be constant. According to Schrupp and Gjerde (1953), teachers tend to see behavior problems from a clinical standpoint more readily than they did three or four decades ago, however, little change has occurred in their ratings of problems. Wickman's (1928) study lists a set of serious problems which remained the chief problems in a survey of teachers 25 years later, and are relatively unchanged today. Thirty-two percent of the teachers studied in 1927 considered undesirable personality traits as one of the more serious problems, and thirty-one percent of the teachers studied 25 years later held the same view.

TYPES OF CONDUCT PROBLEMS

Problems of conduct have been categorized by various authorities. Generally, two criteria have been used: frequency of occurrence and seriousness. Classification of cases of misbehavior by either the criterion of frequency of occurrence or teacher judgments of seriousness has not yielded a theoretical or practical approach. Yet some system of classification is desirable. If each case is a class in itself, then it would allow that there would be at least as many ways of handling behavior problems as there are cases. Recently efforts have been made to reduce the complexity of problems to manageable categories.

This chapter categorizes and examines potential problem areas which may contribute to student misbehavior. These areas include teacher caused misbehavior, student caused misbehavior, family caused misbehavior, and administration caused misbehavior. Misbehavior represents a situation of lack of rapport between the expected or ideal behavior and the actual or real behavior of individuals. All children misbehave at times, but only occasionally is misbehavior regarded as a problem.

Teacher Caused Misbehavior

The teacher brings to the classroom the physiology of a brain, a developmental history, a store of cognitive information, interpersonal relations, sensory input, emotional and psychological needs and affective experience. These factors form the personality of the teacher. Every minute of every waking hour, the personality of an individual reacts to people and to his surroundings. Unfortunately, his environment and personality are always competing with each other; what the individual wants and what his environment will allow are entirely different. This results in a struggle between the two. Reactions are usually laid down by years of experiences engrained by habit. Whether personality conflict and environmental conflict are solved by fleeing, fighting, or compromise, it is important that the teacher understand the factors that cause student misbehavior in the classroom.

The teacher cannot be an effective agent for learning in the classroom unless he has the active cooperation and participation of students. *Rigidity or the inability to be flexible* in any form usually creates problems. Boddel Johnson, a recent graduate of State University with an M.A., wanted to teach at the local community college. Unfortunately, there was no place for him, nor were there any high school positions available in the area. Johnson did secure a position at the local middle school, however. Upon entering the classroom, Johnson felt confident that it would be only a matter of time until he would work his way up through the ranks to the local community college. Johnson's compulsion to cover ground and insistence on high achievement took its toll in student tolerance. He saw his advancement to the community college in terms of academic recognition. Academic recognition to Johnson meant developing a reputation requiring large amounts of outside preparation. Unfortunately, this did not work out. Strict repression of physical activity produced tension. Restriction of movement and constant reminders that deviations in expected behavior would not be tolerated caused Johnson's classroom soon to become chaotic. Teacher insistence that each pupil work quickly and at the same rate of speed can cause undesirable reactions among students. Regulation by the clock coupled with the constant emphasis upon the shortness of time broke Johnson's student rapport.

On the other hand, *too little mature adult leadership* can cause confusion and inappropriate behavior. Shirley Hall was basically an insecure person. The pupils in her class soon learned that an invitation to dinner, kind remarks about her teaching ability, or other words of praise won them good grades. Within six months it was common knowledge that Miss Hall was a "pushover." Hall was overtly defensive to the principal when he talked with any of her students "whom she had adopted as her own."

Pupils often sense a teacher's weakness, play upon it, and then become frustrated as the weakness becomes apparent. Adult maturity is essential to good teaching and learning. When a teacher is pleasant but weak, there is usually a feeling of ambiguity among students. As a result they may feel guilty and conform to the wishes of the teacher to cover their more negative behavior. *Vacillating leadership* is defined as undefined leadership. The teacher does not define what is expected of the student. Consequently, the student is continually groping for clues as to what the boundaries are.

Student expectations are a necessary part of good leadership. Joe Kelly resents authority. His dad "never spared the rod." Kelly has been teaching at Baxter, Neb., Elementary School for five months. Kelly's principal follows the same philosophy of "spare the rod and spoil the child." On one occasion, the principal embarrassed him when he reported late for faculty meeting. Now Kelly holds a grudge against the principal. When a student breaks a school rule, such as throwing paper on the grounds, Kelly covers up for him. Kelly has become an ally of the students against the principal. When students break one of Kelly's rules, however, Kelly is there to defend his rule. Students are confused and frustrated by teacher vacillation. There needs to be a visible set of limits which are plausible, generally consistent and understood by all the students. Effective leadership and discipline require that regulations be uniform and evenly enforced.

Theodore White is teaching for the first time and has secured a position at Conner High School. White is overwhelmed by loneliness and the large city in which he is living. At this point in his life he has little sexual or social contacts. He is intrigued by the sexual lives of others, especially as revealed in magazine articles and books. White has always had an ear for gossip and stories told in the teacher's lounge. Marlene, an attractive 16-year-old junior, lives with her divorced mother. White has heard interesting sexual rumors about divorced women and was awestruck recently by the sophistication and beauty of Marlene's mother. He has even had sexual fantasies about Marlene's mother. Now, he begins to inquire more and more about the life of Marlene's mother. He wants to know her habits, her social life, and he asks detailed intimate questions.

White has become a psychological voyeurist. This is one of a wide range of *personality quirks* that can hinder teacher relations with students. On the other extreme, there are teachers who are almost without feeling for students and too impersonal. They have never felt ready to express themselves about personal matters and cannot tolerate listening to the students who do. They are unwilling to give of themselves emotionally and do not wish to become involved in any kind of human relationship. The need of the student for social communication with the teacher is sacrificed to the teacher's inadequacies. The teacher also may be too dictatorial. This kind of teacher is the kind of person who needs to play God. He is ready to dictate profound decisions and pronounce ultimatums.

Not only can personality oddities cause misbehavior but *personality clashes* can cause even greater problems. Clashes are defined as that point in time at which the personalities of two individuals refuse to yield to the wishes or feelings of the other and it becomes a time at which these personalities feel they must damage or destroy.

Students often draw upon the teacher for a model in organizing their own work load. Marcia Fincher is a second year teacher at Pleasant Hill School. Marcia for the most part is insecure generally and particularly feels the need to explore subject matter in great detail. Students in her classroom often do not bring in their assignments. Fincher usually begins the day with a plan in mind to provide each class with a reasonable amount of time. Unfortunately, Fincher becomes so involved in her first class that it usually lasts all day. Frantically, 30 minutes before the final bell, she rushes madly through her other five classes, making assignments and collecting papers. When students fail to have their assignments the next day Fincher becomes very upset. Students consider her a scatter brain and very *disorganized.*

Subject area skills are essential to maintaining order and discipline. Nothing causes a loss of confidence more quickly than for the students to discover the teacher is uncertain or unfamiliar with the subject material. For instance, Joe Brown was just recently hired by a comprehensive high school as an electronics instructor. Brown has recently experienced a disappointing layoff from a radio equipment testing job and is resorting to teaching as a temporary appointment between jobs. He has a working knowledge of electronics but is unfamiliar with theory and the application of certain theories to specific problems. Students soon discover that Brown is insecure in his subject matter. He spends a great deal of his waking hours off the job seeking new employment and devotes little time to out-of-class preparation. Consequently, much of his class time is devoted to lecture or reading from a textbook. He allows no time for class experimentation and exploration. Two problems in Brown's behavior contribute to misbehavior in the classroom. He has an unfavorable attitude toward the school, students, and staff and he views the school as temporary support while he is trying for something better. He sees teachers as people who "couldn't make it anywhere else." Coupled with his lack of subject matter skill, Brown is soon forced to cope with extreme discipline problems created by students who meet his hostility with open rebellion and his lack of skill with contrived questions designed to cause him embarrassment before the class and his supervisors.

Some teachers have a tendency to *stereotype students*. This can create misbehavior and cause resentment within the student. For example, Dean Coswell recently moved to the West coast to a new teaching position. There he views his students in three categories' white students, black students, and Mexican migrant workers. He has the highest regard for all white students, encourages them, establishes good rapport, and regards them as the leaders of tomorrow. The Mexican and black students are stereotyped and categorized in his mind as trouble makers. To these students, Coswell is cool, aloof, nonsupportive, and most receive failing grades. These students as a result of Coswell's behavior band together to create discipline problems for him.

Most social organizations develop a chain of command. Whether the organization be a police department, army, government organization, or church, members are called upon to recognize authority. *Teachers should not exceed their authority.* The school is no exception. Colonel Abraham Blackwell, retired U.S. Army, sought a second career in the classroom. Blackwell graduated recently with an Ed.S. in administration and is now seeking a principalship. Before potential employers would consider Blackwell, they insisted he gain some classroom experience. Blackwell was recently employed as a seventh grade teacher at Highland Elementary with the understanding he would be promoted when a vacancy occurred in the system. Blackwell was assigned to a principal who had been a former platoon sergeant in his company in Germany. Principal Mullins had a burning dislike for Blackwell. Blackwell felt equally hostile for Mullins because of past events. Blackwell accepted the position with reservation, pledging to himself to prove Mullins inadequate and incompetent on the job. Students in the school soon capitalized on the hostility that existed between Mullins and Blackwell. Highland Elementary became a battleground between the two men and the spoils of war went to the students who laughed at the feud between the two men. It was only a matter of time before both were released from the system.

Students also capitalize on *threats by teachers which are not followed through.* Grace Ireland, a 43-year-old mother of one and 10-year veteran in the classroom, is a 4th-grade teacher. Ireland has a tendency to philosophize and say that each generation of children she teaches is getting worse. She complains about a lack of respect for teachers and bemoans what she labels "the sorry state of affairs." Emotionally, Ireland's husband no longer finds her very attractive and has turned his attention elsewhere. Ireland has transferred her plight to society and blames society in general and the school in particular for her emotional hunger. Ireland makes threats to her students throughout the day and fails to follow through. Her students soon learn that she will take no action and regard her as "battle-axe." "Class," she says, "we are going to have to maintain discipline or I am going to call your parents and tell them you cannot come back."

There are at least twelve reasons for teacher caused misbehavior. These are: rigid leadership; too little adult leadership; vacillating leadership; personality quirks (Morse and Wingo, 1969); personality clashes; disorganization; weak in skill areas; cool and aloof; unfavorable attitude toward school and teaching (Blair, Jones & Simpson, 1975); stereotyping of students; teachers exceeding authority; and no follow-up on discipline.

Student Caused Misbehavior

Research data regarding disruptive misbehavior makes it clear that student caused misbehavior stems from many sources and represents a complexity of facts that reside within and without the student. Seven of these factors will be considered here: the student's unmet needs, his inability to cope with the situation; contagion, composition of the group (Morse and Wingo, 1969) peer group standards, social cliques and physically disabled or mentally handicapped students.

Abraham H. Maslow (Chapter 4), developed a theory of personality which focused on the psychiatrically healthy man. In contrast to many personality theories, especially those in the Freudian tradition, which are primarily concerned with pathology, Maslow argued for a reorientation to a concern for a formulation built around the positive view of man. The structural position of this holistic theory parallels the Gestalt-organismic theories. Although he did not elaborate a theory of developmental sequences, Maslow recognized that the young organism is dominated by physiological and tissue needs. As the organism matures, the needs for safety and security increase, and among these needs are the needs for attention and love. If these *needs are not met,* student misbehavior may result. Students often seek out ways to gain attention at the expense of order in the classroom.

A second source of student sparked misbehavior may be their *inability to cope.* An entire class can ignite a riot when tensions mount to the breaking point. It may occur in a group where none of the students are rabble-rouser types, nor would have started a feud. For instance, a middle school 8th-grade class switched from traditional language arts to the linguistic approach in the middle of the academic year. The teacher, unfamiliar with the material, underexplained and overdemanded from her students. Consequently, the students who had been achievers were now failures and unable to cope with the situation. One day the entire class refused to work. Fortunately, the teacher and principal sensed the problem in time to adapt a slower and more fruitful approach.

Contagion, a nebulous and vague element, can move a group to enthusiasm or hostility. Contagion can be the cause of student misbehavior. The goal of a group may originate with one person or with a few, but in most groups there are leaders who influence others (Redl, 1966). The second component of contagion is ease of communication among members; barriers are broken down and communication spreads like a flood. Such communication is often nonverbal. It may be a gesture, a nod, a show of resistance or some other form of nonverbal communication. Students in groups may become giggly, hilarious, mimicky, and the result is a low efficiency level. Redl (1966) found that there are many variables involved in contagion including type of behavior, group solidarity, degree of frustration, group configuration, and method of leadership. He found that when emotional tones are appropriate unfavorable behavior responses spread rapidly from student to student. Dissatisfaction with classroom activities such as underexplaining a problem or overassignment of work can cause defiance of authority.

The *composition of a group* of students may cause difficulty. Wide differences in age, ability, background, and general achievement make it more difficult to involve students in similar activities. All children need to learn self-control and cooperation with others, but mismatching may create strife and discontent within groups. The tolerance level of many students may be low for various reasons including physical as well as emotional factors. For instance, John is the only black student in a group of ten white female students in the 4th-grade class working on a unit on American Indians. The female students tend to bond together ignoring John. John feels hostile because they will not let him join the group.

The *peer group* serves to motivate students in at least four ways: (1) it forces conformity; (2) easily adapts itself to processes such as discussion and participation; (3) it brings together children who can learn from each other; and, (4) it furnishes a laboratory for learning. The group sets no formal assignments, makes no formal evaluation, and presents no formal plans. It does, nonetheless, assign, evaluate, and plan in a very real way. This is accomplished through a complex system of recognitions, rewards, and status within the social structure of the group. When a student meets or exceeds the standards of the group, certain rewards are bestowed upon that student. If classmates frown on unruly behavior, a student will soon learn to behave in an approved manner. Berenda (1950) reported that there was a great deal of acquiescing to majority opinion even when the majority was known to be wrong. Asch (1951) substantiates Berenda's findings. Festinger and others (1950) discovered that intergroup communication was directed toward individuals who were the most divergent and that great pressure was exerted to get them to align their opinions with group standards.

A *social clique* may arise when groups bond together for certain reasons. For instance, certain clubs gain or achieve social status within the school by influencing selected students. Popular social cliques, through influence of its members, gain certain concessions within the school community as well as the social community. Consequently, students may actively campaign to become members of a social clique and teachers and principals may at the same time wish to gain the support of a social clique for reasons of order and professional approval from students and parents.

Physically disabled and mentally handicapped students present the teacher with a far greater problem in coping with misbehavior. There are children born with motor dysfunction exhibited by poor body function. This may be evident in their gait or in poor coordination in throwing a ball or working a puzzle. Other children may exhibit special neurological limitation in the way they respond to their environment. Difficulty may arise in stimuli (perception), in organizing, storing, and patterning information they take in and in the expression of their feelings and ideas.

Family Caused Misbehavior

The teacher harvests the products of the formative years and early development in students. There is a complex configuration of factors to study regarding the sources of family caused misbehavior. Some of these are: the effects of birth order, of parental rejection, of mother or father dominated families, of divorce, of anxious parents, of striving parents, of lower-class families, of urban living, of ethnic groups. This section will examine eight possible causes of family initiated misbehavior: parents who see no need for education, parents who abuse children, parents who neglect and abandon children, parents who blame children for their lack of success, extreme pressures placed on children by parents, migratory status of parents, divorced parents, and parents who view the school in terms of a babysitting service.

Parents often see no need for education.

Parents who see no need for education are constantly degrading school and placing educators in an undesirable light. For instance, William Kelley, 45-year-old contractor, only completed the 3rd grade. Kelley entered construction work immediately following the Korean Conflict and seems to "have the touch of King Midas." Kelley has three children and constantly reminds them of his success without an education. He proudly points out that a person with a doctorate at the local college only makes $17,000 in twelve months while he can make that much on three houses in four months. All his children are potential drop-outs, because they see little value in education. Kelley rewards deviant behavior because he sees it as a way for his children to "get even with school officials for making my kids go to school." "I need them on the job."

The rising incidents of *child abuse and abandonment* have alarmed many civic leaders and educators. A young girl and her smaller brother, both victims of child abuse, were recently discovered in a large city adjacent to a medical school. The girl's leg was broken and her body revealed multiple cuts and bruises from a severe beating. Her brother was also in critical condition. In the same city, a new born baby was discovered in a trash container near the city hall. Various reasons have been offered to explain these situations; however, none of them take away the emotional and psychological scars left on the individual. A student abused by his parents may see the classroom as a place of escape or retaliation. Children are abandoned

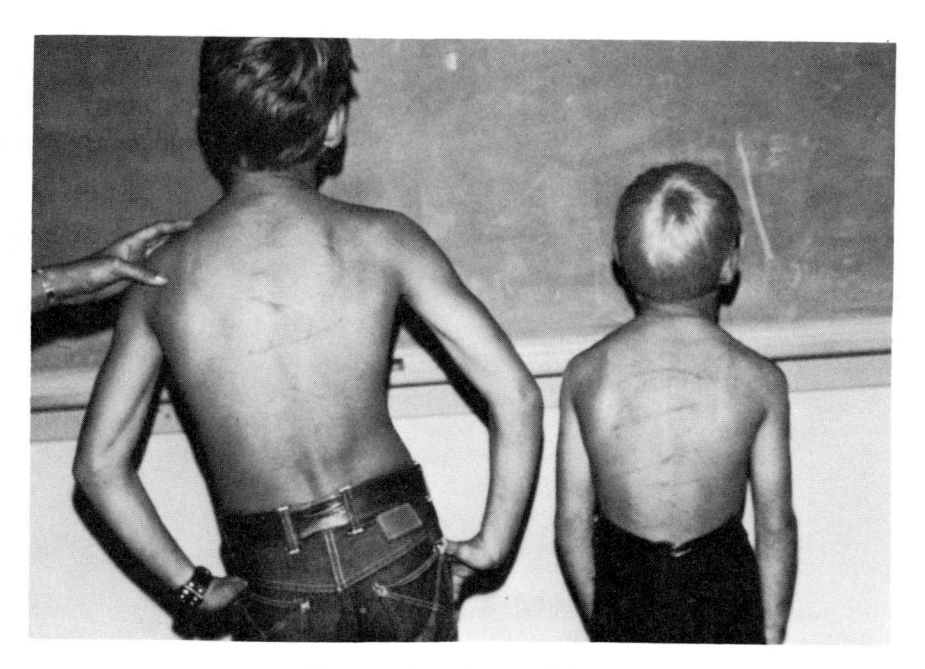

Parents often abuse children.

for many reasons. These range from emotional to economic reasons. Children are beaten and abused for similar reasons. A parent may blame an unwanted child for his "bad luck," or the child may serve as a scapegoat for the venting of the parents' anger.

Parents have different ways of abusing children; psychological abuse may be as detrimental as physical abuse. For instance, John and Mildred Brown were both premedical students at a small college. When twins were born to the couple, both had to drop out of college and John had to go to work at the local clothing factory. After the twins, four children were born in rapid succession. Their financial situation went from bad to worse. Now it is a meager existence at best and John especially blames the children for his lack of success. Often he sees his children as stumbling blocks to a better economic situation and the children are treated as social and economic burdens. *John blames the children for his lack of success.* "They are just mouths to feed," Brown often mutters to himself.

On the other side of the coin, *extreme pressure can be placed on children* by parents because of their position in life or society, because of their own frustrated ambitions, and over-emphasis on education. For example, Jim Jones, a 4th-grade drop-out always wanted to be an attorney. He came from a very poor family and had to go to work at an early age to support his mother, for his father had died of cancer when he was 14. Jones's

Divorced parents contribute to misbehavior.

son is now in high school and vitally interested in electronics. The son is a "ham operator" and builds many electronic components: Jones, on the other hand, is determined for his son to go to college to study law. Rebellion is currently brewing. Signs of an upcoming revolution against Jim Jones are now surfacing. For instance, his son slashed the tires of a police car recently. He laughed over the fact that his father had to hire a lawyer at a very high fee to get "me out of trouble." In the classroom Jones, Jr., is constantly rebelling against authority figures such as the teacher and principal.

When students are uncertain of parental expectation or when these expectations are inconsistent, misbehavior may result. Jenny Smithfield's *parents divorced* several years ago. Jenny spends six months with her mother and six months with her father. The personalities are completely different. Her mother is stern and demanding while her father is relaxed and exerts no discipline. Jenny is frustrated and confused about what is expected of her. She can date and stay out late while she is with her father, but her mother forbids dating. As the tension mounts, her behavior in the classroom reflects her apprehension about life.

Some parents may see the school as a *"baby-sitting"* service.

"Damn it, Ben, why are they closing school today?"

"Ben you know what this means. If I don't report for work today we'll lose the second car." "Damn, Damn, Damn."

This conversation occurred between Ben and Martha Staton. This young couple live well beyond their means of two incomes. The school is seen as a baby-sitting service. Ben and Martha usually deliver their children at the school door an hour before the first bell and pick them up after all other students have gone home. The Staton children are near exhaustion by the end of the day.

Migratory parents who move with the crop harvest present a special problem to the maintenance of discipline within the classroom. Students constantly on the move are not able to establish feelings of identification with a community and are unable to develop lasting friendships. Moreover, living conditions for these children are often very poor. They may live in the back of a truck or under other very poor housing conditions.

Administration Caused Misbehavior

Sources of administration caused misbehavior stem from an over emphasis on the external control of students in response to an unhealthy community attitude toward students; difference in the philosophy of the administration and faculty; and, vague teacher authority.

It is not uncommon to find administrators, fearing disorganization, *over controlling students.* This is at a time when students need to be learning to control their own behavior. Problems arise when there is an excess of external control as opposed to self-discipline. Teachers are treated in very formal ways, and each visitor to the school may be required to get personal permission from the principal's office before entering the school. Usually, instruction is conducted on a very formal basis. Teachers may acquire a strong custodial sense as they lose their humanitarian feelings for students.

Unfortunately, in some cases young people and subcultures within the youth community have been presented by the news media as being in a state of rebellion. Too often, civic and community leaders have accepted this judgment. Consequently, all youth are seen by adults and school leaders, who *reflect community judgments,* as being hostile, destructive and a menace to the community social structure. This stereotyped attitude is unfair. Adolescents do develop a stylized hostility toward adults on occasion, but this occurs generally because they are trying to become adults more rapidly than society allows them to assume adult roles.

When *administration and faculty differ in their philosophical outlook,* misbehavior may develop in students because students tend to play one side of authority against the other for their own goals. For example, Mike Henry, a recent graduate from State University, received his M.A. degree in administration and is now to assume the role of principal at Redan High School. Henry comes to a school with a long tradition of strict rules and orderly movement within the school. The retiring principal prides himself on the order in his school when comparing his school to those of his colleagues who have experienced racial strife. Unfortunately, the students from Redan High School have not been successful in self-discipline. An alarming number of those students after leaving Redan have been arrested for various law violations. Usually, officers report it to be a "lack of self-control."

Henry was determined to bring some needed changes to Redan. His first order of business was to change completely policy and procedure. Because of the popularity of the former principal among the faculty, Henry became the target of the faculty's anger. They refer to the new principal as the man with the "funny new ideas." They perceive these new "ideas" as being destructive to Redan's tradition. It was unfortunate that Henry did not take the time to prepare the faculty and students for his change in administration. It was not long before students were taking full advantage of Henry's liberal policy and chaos was the order of the day. Henry was soon replaced.

Another problem of misbehavior arises when *teacher authority is vague*. Some principals see teachers as having the same need for discipline as students, and see their job as being one of line supervision. This is directly opposed to what ASCD of the National Education Association states as the purpose and definition of supervision. Supervision and administration is conceptualized as being a cooperative endeavor. The time of "snoopervision" is well passed.

Jesse Jonston, principal of Allgood Elementary School, is 54 and a graduate of State Teacher's College. Jonston has always reprimanded teachers on the spot. When students create an excessive amount of noise in the lunch room, he makes it a point to create an embarrassing situation so the teacher appears incompetent. This is a control device for Jonston. Jonston seldomly provides discipline support for teachers.

SOLUTIONS TO MISBEHAVIOR PROBLEMS

All four areas of student misbehavior—teacher caused, student caused, family caused, administration caused—may be corrected. It should be noted, however, that any substantive accomplishment in correcting any area of student misbehavior must begin with the teacher.

Solutions to Teacher Caused Misbehavior Problems

Many beginning teachers will *need experience* before they can distinguish clearly between what misbehavior should be overlooked and what should be dealt with. The teacher who makes an issue out of each whisper is not a mature, effective teacher. It is difficult to distinguish between forms of problem behavior which will become worse if the teacher ignores them and those which will become worse if he draws attention to them.

Behavior that can safely be ignored in one situation may signal real trouble in another instance. The particular means that a teacher employs are not nearly as important as the manner in which he approaches the problem of discipline. Often how he says and does it reveals to the student his actual motivations as well as his own confidence or uncertainty.

Inadequate relationships on the part of the teacher may be the result of defensive reactions to cover up personal insecurity. Reasons for the insecurity may be simple and relatively obvious, or they may be complex and deep. There is no easy way to erase insecurity; however, it may be possible to bring it under conscious control. A teacher who is ready to take a frank look at what he is doing and what he is feeling will find the following helpful solutions to teacher caused misbehavior.

Teachers can learn a great deal from *pupil evaluation*. In fact, all teachers should routinely and systematically seek student evaluation of their work, judgments about the curriculum, group relationships, and individual pupil behavior. It is not always easy for a teacher to ask his students to tell how they feel about the way the teacher relates to them, but it can be rewarding and informative.

Self-evaluation is also important to good discipline. New teachers and dedicated career teachers occasionally find themselves under pressures requiring self-study. Self-understanding may be augmented by readings, courses, and seminars. Some teachers have found training or sensitivity groups helpful in complementing the awareness gained from self-study. Candid discussion of the way one behaves in the group, the feelings generated, and the attitudes expressed can enable a person to change his behavior.

Personal therapy may be beneficial. Whenever the cause of a teacher's problem-creating behavior lies in personal problems, he may need therapy. There are teachers who have grown up unable to accept children and youth adequately. Stress brought about by certain life cycles such as those related to marriage, divorce, one's own children, menopause, or death may require therapy. Clinical work with teachers suggests that personal strain is a source of difficulty often ignored. A persistent physiological pain sends us to the physician, whereas we hesitate to seek the aid of a psychologist for a persistent psychological pain.

Frank discussion with other teachers can be useful. Sometimes discussion means nothing more than common sharing of problems. Approached with purpose, however, it can be a way to understand how others have handled certain pupils they did not like or certain conditions that irritated them. Open *discussion with supervisory personnel* can be enlightening and revealing. Fear of authority sometimes makes it difficult for a teacher to go to the person in charge and ask for help. Nor do all authorities want to hear of trouble.

Slobetz (1950) shows how teachers met classroom behavior problems. The following table gives an outline of his results.

How Situations Were Met	Frequency
Physical force (spanked, shook, tied in seat, etc)	1%
Censure (scolded, warned, shamed, hushed, etc.)	11%
Overtime or extra work	5%
Deprivation (deprived recreational time, etc.)	10%
Sent or referred to office	.06%
Penalties (demerits, money fines, nonpromotion)	1%
Rectification or reparation	2%
Ignored or did nothing	5%
Verbal appeal	25%
Group reaction	1%
Constructive assistance	31%
Commendation	.06%
Search for reason of behavior	6%
Tried many things unsuccessfully	.03%

The teacher should plan on a weekly or bi-weekly basis. By *preplanning* many misbehavior problems are eliminated because misbehavior results most frequently when curricular shifts take place. Preplanning provides for smooth transitions from one content area to another. It also gives the teacher an opportunity to collect materials and reflect on learning difficulties of students.

Some other solutions to misbehavior problems are:

1. Strengthen weak skill and academic areas by enrolling in courses at a college or university.
2. Tempers should cool before administering punishment. When tempers flare hot and heavy, responses may not be rational.
3. The teacher must be aware of student's rights and responsibilities as well as his own. Current developments in individual rights have brought many changes in this area.
4. The teacher should be fair and consistent in administering punishments and rewards. The teacher often serves as a model for pupil concept development in this area.
5. Effective classroom guidelines are those developed cooperatively between the teacher and the student. Practice in decision making and participation in a democratic environment will foster good citizenship and often draw the student into desirable behavior patterns.

6. The teacher should seek the level of employment with which he feels most comfortable. For example, some teachers experience great difficulty in working with students in early childhood.
7. If all else fails after applying these solutions, perhaps a reassessment of the teacher's work-life is in order.

Teachers should create a *healthy milieu*. Even when specialists are available to work intensively with disturbed children a few hours a week, the many other hours spent in school each week exert a continuing influence. Unless thought is given to making this influence a supportive and integrative one, the work of the specialists may be in vain.

A major technique available to teachers for dealing with problem behavior is the technique of the *conference interview*. Although talk is not a solution in itself, the teacher, through talking, can collect information, try out his judgments of what is wrong and what should be done, develop rapport, and exert influence. The purposes of the interview vary widely. Ideally, it is a teaching and a learning experience for both the teacher and the pupil. An interview is an opportunity for student and teacher to inquire together about the student's feelings, attitudes, behavior, and problems, and about their consequences.

Behavior may be improved by *providing models*. Teachers, peers, older children, parents, status figures, and even heroes in films and books serve as models for behavior. Putting models to use constructively in the school is another matter. How one group of teachers accomplished this is described by Hicks (1967) who arranged for one group of older students in a predominantly black junior high school in East St. Louis, Missouri, to serve as teachers for younger pupils during a period of several weeks. Behavior problems in both the older and the younger pupils were reduced and attitudes toward school were improved.

Undesirable behavior also may be eliminated by *not rewarding* it. A clear and simple example is provided by Charles H. Madsen, Jr., and Clifford K. Madsen (1970). A teacher was bothered at her desk by students who were coming to the front of the room unnecessarily. There were twenty-eight occurrences of this behavior in one week. In response, the teacher ignored all the children who came to the desk. She made no eye contact with them and said nothing. She recognized only those children who raised their hands at their seats. After two weeks the number of children who unnecessarily came to the teacher's desk dropped from twenty-eight to zero.

Teachers should *use punishment sparingly and wisely*. Punishment can have many undesirable side effects, and at the same time not be very effective in controlling behavior. The importance of involving the peer group in the formation of rules and the use of presenting painful stimulation—namely, fines—as a sanction to back up the rule is a viable alternative to corporal punishment.

Solutions to Student Caused Misbehavior

There are a variety of influences and techniques a teacher can apply to change the course of events in student caused misbehavior. For example, Redle and Wattenbert (1959) suggest various techniques that can be applied when it looks certain that a child will no longer effectively control his behavior, but before the limit is actually reached. In recent years the increased problems in control have brought about a great deal of discussion about possible solutions to student caused misbehavior. For instance, the use of corporal punishment at home and at school has become a controversial subject. It has been argued that many children experience physical punishment at home and thus it is expected at school.

Appropriate instructional goals mean *meeting the needs of students.* The first road the teacher should pursue in trouble-shooting is to check curriculum demands against the actual capacity of the pupils. To disregard pupils' readiness in planning activities and choosing materials is to invite trouble.

Occasionally, discipline problems are caused by *physical discomfort.* Poor lighting, crowded conditions, uncomfortable furniture, or too many restrictions on moving about all may contribute to undesirable behavior patterns on the part of the student.

Improved communication with children and adolescents is paramount in solving discipline problems. How does the stalemate in communication between the school and the student come about? First of all, the stalemate happens because teachers do not know their students. Some valid generalizations and suggestions for keeping discipline are:

1. Understand the peer group, thereby understanding the student as a part of his environment.
2. Give children the responsibility of self-discipline.
3. Challenge the group in order to increase group cohesiveness.
4. Reduce the effect of social cliques on individual students.
5. Gain the respect of the student's peer group and use it to control behavior.
6. Individualize teaching.
7. When a student misbehaves, he should be studied in an effort to determine which of his needs has been neglected.
8. Reexamine your own expectations.

When group morale and behavior do not reach expectations, the teacher can turn to group discussion. Experts agree that such activities may have merit, but often it burdens the class members with decisions requiring insight and objectivity about human nature which they are not yet prepared to handle. A more feasible course of action may be for teacher and students to share the responsibility for dealing with problems that involve them all. The technique of allowing the group to discuss grievances under adult guidance is often called *"ventilation"* (Morse and Wingo, 1969). A prerequuisite to this process requires a generally permissive attitude so that students will feel free to vent their feelings about classroom conditions.

Role playing can help locate the source of the trouble. Through acting the parts of other persons, the participants and the observers as well gain insight into the dynamics of human relations. They may see their own and others' actions and attitudes in new perspective. For the teacher, it is an opportunity to gain insight into the feelings and problems of the students, for children often voice their fears and frustrations while pretending to be someone else. Two requirements must be observed while carrying on the process. The problems acted out must be relevant to real-life experiences and significant to a majority of the group. And the teacher must be willing to allow the pupils to explore the problem and interpret the roles as they wish.

Breaking up a group may be an aid to solving misbehavior problems. Often disruptive behavior will not spread through a whole group if the unit is divided. Subgroups provide barriers to overall communication and the disturbances can be isolated. Action requiring a large audience is not very desirable in such a situation; the student who clowns in front of forty students may find his behavior unrewarding in a small group.

It is important to develop *appropriate expectations.* Students engaged in worthwhile activities they find challenging are likely to be developing the know-how of effective self-management. When children spend their time doing busy work, trouble generally results. Checking on one's expectations is a good place to begin in finding a solution to discipline problems. A teacher can also analyze whether or not his own level of expectation is realistic.

Solutions to Family Caused Misbehavior

The general conditions existing in homes from which children come have been shown by research to have marked effects on children's behavior and personality. The effects of parental discipline on personality characteristics in children have been the subject of speculation; however, only a modest amount of factual evidence exists. Three tentative conclusions can be drawn from the available research data:

1. Harsh discipline may build a store of hostility that the child directs toward others.

2. There is a positive relationship between aggressive behavior in children and the severity of discipline in the home.
3. Strict discipline by parents often leads to prejudiced and antidemocratic attitudes in the child.

Additional evidence of the effect of family influences on personality has been found in research on delinquency. One such study, Jenkins and Glickman (1947) identified three types of delinquent children, (1) an unsocialized aggressive group, (2) a socialized delinquent group, and (3) an emotionally disturbed delinquent group. The unsocialized aggressive boys usually came from homes where they had experienced parental rejection; the socialized delinquents were better accepted at home than the aggressive delinquents and came from larger families, but they were reared under family conditions involving extremely slack discipline.

Reporting to parents on students' progress has been a controversial topic for many years. Conventional report cards have been attacked. Some critics have even proposed the elimination of all evaluation reports' regardless of the form used. Usually the argument has been that evaluation reports ruin the sensitive child and place a stigma on the academically slow child. Reporting may be a way, however, of improving communications and thus improving discipline.

Attention has been focused on certain problems involved in the use of check lists as a means of reporting students' progress to parents. The main difficulty lies in lack of precise evidence on which the teacher bases the generalization expressed by the check mark. Parents like to receive both written and oral reports on their children's progress. Because the child is in a different environment at school from that at home, the teacher may see facets of the child's personality and character that are not obvious to the parents. The reverse also is true. Teachers and parents need to share information for the mutual benefit of the student.

Other steps teachers may take include:

1. Reporting parental abuse;
2. Trying to reduce parental pressure on the child;
3. Making school interesting to the student by stressing and developing his interests;
4. Making education life-like;
5. Visiting the home; and,
6. Referring to the guidance department for more information.

Solutions to Administration Caused Misbehavior

It is the job of the school administration to help society understand the school and to attempt to bring to a consensus educators' thinking and public thinking. The administration bears the brunt of society's scrutiny and must answer for the performance of individual staff. This gives added impetus to the administration's regular evaluation of instructional goals.

Reserve support is the availability of aid from outside the classroom. Teachers often say that if they have it they do not need it. On the other hand, if they do not have back-up support, it may become critical. This is because students who realize there is no higher authority will often exploit the teacher's lack of power.

It is essential that the *principal be fully aware of current events in the school.* This means that he does not blindly back a teacher. He acts for what are basically reasonable mores for the school culture. He helps the pupil and the teacher sort out values and motivations. It generally helps the pupil and the teacher to understand any errors they have made in conduct, expectations and requests of the other individual. There may be a great deal of anxiety about saving face on the part of the adults. The pupil's need to save face is seldom considered. In reality, there is no place for face saving because the object should be to work out a reasonable solution to the difficulty as it comes to be understood.

Additional solutions include:

1. Discussing problems with department heads who will communicate with the principal;
2. Discussing as a faculty, with the principal, problems related to student misbehavior;
3. Using professional leave days for observation in other schools in the area;
4. Talking over problems with the principal on a professional level and trying to reach a compromise; and,
5. After exhausting all other methods, seriously consider a transfer.

CURRENT RESEARCH

Representative research efforts in misbehavior problems include studies on changing children's beliefs about punishment (Jensen and Rytting, 1975); discipline, what can we teach (Snider and Murphy, 1975); humanitarianism and corporal punishment (McCarthy, 1975); and, experienced and expected problems reported by families after a family move (Schaller, 1974).

Jensen and Rytting (1974) studied 42 middle-class preschool children who were assigned to either reinforcement, discussion, or control groups in the context of moral training about restitutive punishments. Students in the reinforcement groups were presented with nine stories each day for five days; after subjects had expressed their view on the appropriate punishment for the characters depicted in the stories, a female E reinforced (with poker chips) those subjects who had identified a restitutive punishment. In the discussion group, the children heard five similar stories and, following a short discussion, E continued with the next story without telling the subjects which was the best punishment and without giving any reinforcement. The experimental individuals heard nonmoral stories. Pretest and posttest measures of moral judgments were secured and a two-month follow-up posttest was conducted. Results from a preliminary and a main experiment showed that children exposed to the various procedures made significantly more mature judgments about punishment on the posttests. There were no differences between the two training groups.

Snider and Murphy (1975) consider characteristics of positive discipline, which by definition is nonpunitive. One characteristic is acceptance, which implies that the teacher respects the child for what he is. Another important characteristic of the study was individual responsibility: the child must take the logical consequences of his behavior choice. A third characteristic of positive discipline is its likeness to reality therapy, which tries to meet the basic psychological needs: to love and be loved, to feel needed, and to be worthwhile to oneself and to others.

McCarthy (1975) discusses some of the effects of verbal corporal punishment directed towards children and offers some suggestions in finding solutions to discipline in the classroom. These recommendations include anticipation of individual student needs, new direction of energy of individual students, and a responsive listening teacher who involves the student in finding a solution to a problem if one is manifested.

Schaller (1974) conducted two studies with a total of 849 fourth graders and 5th graders in compulsory comprehensive schools in Sweden to study children's reaction to a family move. Pupils who had never changed schools had a more negative attitude to a hypothetical move than subjects who had actually changed schools. Students who had attended at least two schools had a more negative attitude to a hypothetical move than they had to the last one they had actually made. Individuals who had moved once or more compared with subjects who had never moved, were more willing to move. Problems of initial adjustment after a family move seemed to influence childrens' readiness to move again. Children who moved a short distance reported fewer worries and adjustment problems than those who moved a long distance. They concluded that both parents and teachers need to be particularly careful of children who change schools.

SUMMARY

The orderly functioning of a school requires discipline. Current emphasis in discipline focuses on self-discipline. This chapter examined misbehavior caused by the teacher, student, parent and administrator. Solutions applicable to the classroom were discussed. Representative articles from current research were presented.

An important concern of the educational psychologist is the teacher's understanding of the nature of intelligence for effective student evaluation. An extensive review of Piaget's theory of cognitive development is given in Chapter 7.

DISCIPLINE
STUDENT OBJECTIVES

In an objective type test which may include matching, multiple choice, and one word answers, the student will be able to:

- (K) 1. Identify Morse and Wingo's definition of discipline.
- (K) 2. Identify the three meanings of discipline.
- (K) 3. List all teacher caused behavior problems.
- (K) 4. List all student caused misbehavior problems.
- (K) 5. List all family caused misbehavior problems.
- (K) 6. List all administratively caused misbehavior problems.
- (C) 7. Give examples of each of the caused misbehavior problems indicated in objectives 3-6.
- (S) 8. Devise solutions to hypothetical misbehavior problems using information from their notes.
- (S) 9. Appraise solutions to hypothetical situations stated above.
- (An) 10. Discriminate between relevant and irrelevant information in diagnosing a behavioral problem situation.
- (Ap-An) 11. Discriminate and demonstrate his/her understanding of caused misbehavior problems by applying the correct solution as indicated by the class notes.
- (E) 12. Critically review a research article on discipline and explain it to the class (summarize).
- (K-C) 13. List and explain all methods of teacher, student, family and administration caused misbehavior.
- (S) 14. Categorize caused misbehavior problems and/or methods of overcoming caused misbehavior problems into the respective categories.
- 15. List three of his/her own reasons as to the applicability of the results, of the study they reviewed.

Chapter 7
STUDENT EVALUATION

It is crucial that a teacher have a knowledge of one area of the student's personality—cognitive development and intelligence. The teacher should familiarize himself with the theories of cognitive development and intelligence. Moreover, the teacher should gain a working knowledge of intelligence testing techniques and achievement tests. A teacher who can make competent use of these concepts and facts can then evaluate the student's potential and even evaluate the causes of inadequate achievement.

INTELLIGENCE

Intelligence is a controversial concept; the exact nature and determinants of intelligence have been debated heatedly over the years, and at the present time are unclear. The controversy continues in this century and has assumed renewed significance with the current focus on mental retardation. It is generally agreed that intelligence represents a person's problem-solving capacities, his adaptability to new situations, his ability to form concepts and to benefit from experience. Consequently, intelligence may be viewed not as static but rather as dynamically changing according to the individual's life circumstances.

Definitions of Intelligence

The difficulty in arriving at a definition of intelligence may account for the unending controversy about the causative factors in the developments in the field. In the early part of the century, the lines were sharply polarized between the advocates of the theory of fixed and genetically predetermined intelligence and those who considered environmental factors the most decisive ones. This nature versus nurture controversy was prolonged, many technological developments and discoveries have provided support for both factions. It is important to note the rapid advances in genetics and increased knowledge of the cell processes, the conceptual model for brain activity provided by information theory and cybernetics, studies of identical twins reared in dissimilar environments, the recognition of the relevance of the obstetrical complications to the functioning of an individual, and the interest in maternal and cultural deprivation. Contemporary views of intelligence move away from extreme definitions and there appears to be a gravitation toward a more synthesized understanding of the concept.

Among the various definitions that have been given are these: the ability to learn, the ability to adjust to one's environment, the ability to do abstract thinking, and the ability to profit by one's experience. All these contribute something to the notion of intelligence. The following definition may be more complete: intelligence is the ability to see and discover relationships, and the ability to utilize present information remembered, imagined, or surmised.

THEORIES OF INTELLIGENCE

In 1900, the Swedish sociologist Key, having waged a successful battle for the emancipation of women, predicted that the 20th century was to be the century of the child. A number of events occurred. State legislatures in Illinois and Colorado had passed statutes in 1899 establishing juvenile courts, in which delinquent children were handled differently from adult offenders. As juvenile courts began to spring up all over the country, some of the judges, eager to learn why the young offenders turned to crime, consulted psychiatrists, who thus were obliged to occupy themselves with children. As a result, Healy founded the Juvenile Psychopathic Institute in 1909 in connection with the Chicago Juvenile Court and published his book, *The Individual Delinquent,* in 1915, a report based on case studies instead of diffuse speculations on delinquency in the abstract.

Intelligence tests were first designed for the school child. At the turn of the twentieth century the minister of Public Instruction in Paris was concerned about which students could attend and succeed in a regular school, and which students needed special instruction. In 1904, Dr. Alfred Binet and Dr. Theodore Simon were charged with the responsibility of identifying ways to distinguish between the bright and not so bright children. Binet believed that the nature of intelligence changes with age, so the two men began to select test items to be graded by both age and difficulty. In administering the test, the examiner finds the age level at which the subject passes all of the tests, called his basal age. Then he continues testing until the subject reaches the age level where not one of the tests is passed or the upper limit. The tests are scored in units of months of mental age. Thus, all tests passed are added to the basal age, and the mental age of the child can be determined.

In 1905, Binet and Simon made public their intelligence scale. It was introduced by Goddard in this country in 1910. Wilhelm Stern and Frederick Kuhlmann in 1912 separately proposed the use of an index or ratio between mental age and chronological age. Terman utilized this idea in his 1916 Stanford-Binet test and developed the concept of intelligence quotient (IQ). These tests now offered a concrete means of helping teachers evaluate a child's ability to grasp classroom instruction. This became the first reliable attempt to prevent educational mismanagement.

As a result, between 1899 and 1909 the scene was set for individual work with problem children. The following decade was mainly one of legislative implementation of some of these insights, a transition from unorganized philanthropy to systematic community endeavors. In 1921, Thom opened the Boston Habit Clinic for the guidance of problem children; in 1922, child guidance clinics were set up in a few communities; in 1930 there were about 500 such clinics, and more than 50 countries sent delegates to the First International Congress of Mental Hygiene in Washington, D.C.

Binet's Theory of Intelligence

In Binet's theory, intelligence is understood as a very complex concern, comprising a number of different abilities, and he supported this conviction by introducing tests of many kinds into his composite scale. He did not know what the component abilities were, although he noted that there were several different kinds of memory, for example. He followed the idea of using a single composite score, because the immediate practical application was to make a single administrative decision regarding each child.

Spearman's Theory of Intelligence

Test-makers who followed Binet were generally unconcerned about having a basic psychological theory for intelligence tests, another instance of technology running far in advance of theory. There was some concern about theory in England, however, where Charles Spearman developed a procedure of factor analysis by which it became possible to discover component abilities. Spearman found that the results of most intelligence tests were highly correlated with each other, and he therefore concluded the existence of "g," or a general factor, to account for the results of his research. Nevertheless, he did observe some differences relating to particular kinds of intelligence test items, such as numerical or verbal. Consequently, he believed that there were also specific factors, or "s," that influenced intellectual tasks. Intelligence, therefore, or more properly, intelligent behavior, is a composite of a general factor that pervades all intellectual activity plus a specific factor or factors relevant to the immediate task. Spearman's model is illustrated in Figure 2.

Thurstone's Theory of Intelligence

Spearman's theory has been challenged most notably by L.L. Thurstone and his students. Utilizing factor analysis techniques, Thurstone studied the results of numerous intelligence test items given to a large number of subjects. He found distinct factors that he called primary mental abilities, rather than a single general factor. Thurstone listed 6 such abilities, although other investigators do not agree on the exact total. The

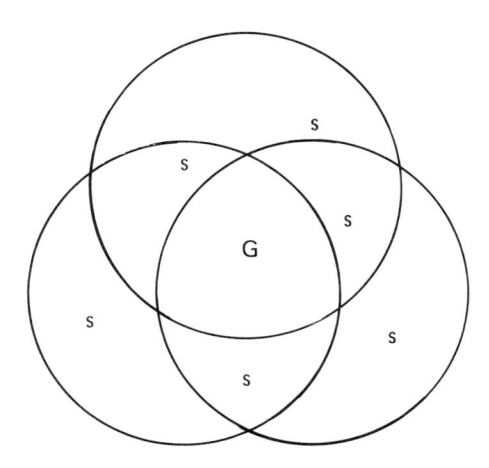

Figure 2. This figure illustrates Spearman's model. Spearman's two factor theory of learning involves the interaction between the general factor (g) and many specific factors (s). The larger the g factor the more intelligent the individual is. Less intelligent individuals possess a larger s factor.

primary mental abilities were; verbal, numbers, spatial, word fluency, memory and reasoning. Factor analyses in the United States have followed almost exclusively the multiple-factor theory of Thurstone, which is more general than Spearman's. In Thurstone's conception, a group factor is not necessary, but analysis by his methods would reveal it if the intercorrelations warrant such a result.

A major source of identified intellectual abilities was the research of aviation psychologists in the U.S. Army Air Force during World War II. More important than the outcome of adding numbers to intellectual abilities, there was now recognition of the fact that where Thurstone had found one spatial ability, there proved to be at least three, one being recognized as spatial orientation and another as spatial visualization. Where Thurstone had found an inductive ability, there were three reasoning abilities.

Another major event was in the form of a program of analyses conducted in the Aptitudes Research Project at the University of Southern California. Begun in 1949, this project focused attention on tests in the provisional categories of reasoning, creative thinking, planning, evaluation, and problem solving. Nearly 20 years later, the number of separate intellectual abilities has increased to about 80, with at least 50% more predicted by a comprehensive unified theory.

Guilford's Theory of Intelligence

Guilford observed that there were a number of parallels between abilities in terms of their common features. Some examples of parallels in abilities will explain this. Two parallel abilities differ in only one respect. There was known to be an ability to see relations between perceived, visual figures, and a parallel ability to see relations between concepts. An example of a test item in the first case would mean seeing that one figure is the lower-left half of another. An item in the second instance might require understanding that the word "bird" is an object while "fly" is its mode of locomotion. The ability to do the one kind of item is relatively independent of the ability to do the other, the only difference being that of informational types—concrete or perceived in the one case and abstract or conceived in the other.

For a pair of abilities differing in another way, the type of information is the same for both. One of the abilities deals with seeing class ideas. Given the set of words "ottoman," "lamp," "rocker," "radio," can the student grasp the essential nature of the class, as shown by his naming the class, by putting another word or two into it, or by recognizing its name among four alternatives? The ability pertains to discovery or recognition of a class concept. In another kind of test the examinee is asked to produce classes by dividing a list of words into mutually exclusive sets, each having a different class concept. These two abilities are independent. One involves a process of understanding and the other a process of production. These processes involve two psychologically different kinds of operations.

A third kind of parallel ability contains pairs that are alike in type of information involved and in kind of operation. For example, suppose the tester gave the student the following: "Name as many objects as you can that are both edible and "green." Here the examiner has given the specifications for a class, and the examinee is to produce from his memory store some class members. The ability involved was first called "ideational fluency." The more appropriate members the examinee can list in a limited time, the better his score. In a test for a parallel ability, instead of producing single words the student is asked to write a list of sentences. To standardize his task for testing purposes and to control his efforts, the first letters of four words that he is to give in each of a variety of sentences is provided for him. For example, W ____ c____ s____ d ____ . Without using any word twice, the examinee may write, "Why can't Sue dance?" "Workers could seldom demand," or "Wondering cows sense destruction." This test differs from the classifying test because in the classifying test, the words given to the examinee are so selected that they form a unique set of classes and the person is so informed. The process is called "convergent production." In the latter two tests under discussion, there are many possible responses and the examinee produces alternatives. This operation is labeled "divergent production." This involves a broad searching or scanning process where both operations depend upon retrieval of information from the student's memory.

The difference between the two abilities illustrated by the last two tests lies in the nature of the items produced. In the first case there are single words that stand for single objects or concepts. The item produced, the "product," is a unit or entity of information. In the second instance, the product is an organized sequence of words, each word representing a concept or unit. This kind of product is called "system."

Guilford's theory is explained by a matrix type of model (see Figure 3). This model shows the differences in the three ways discussed: operation (kind of processing of information), content (kind of information), and product (formal phase of information).

OPERATIONS
  Cognition
  Memory
  Divergent production
  Convergent production
  Evaluation

PRODUCTS
  Units
  Classes
  Relations
  Systems
  Transformations
  Implications

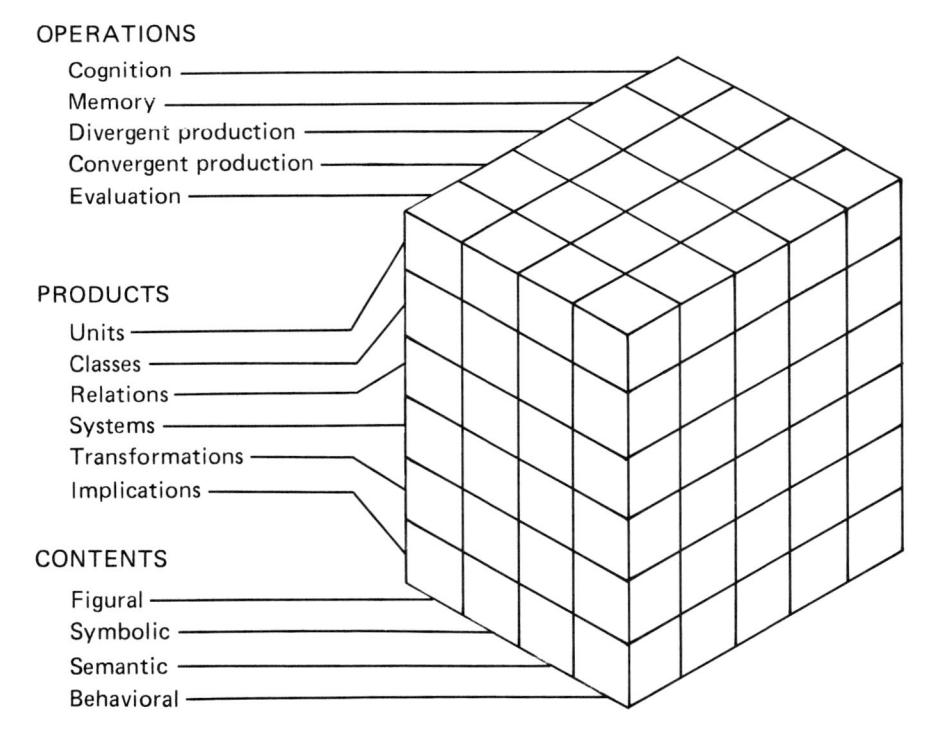

CONTENTS
  Figural
  Symbolic
  Semantic
  Behavioral

Figure 3. Guilford's matrix type model. J.P. Guilford's "Intelligence 1965 Model," *American Psychologist,* Vol. 21, 1966, p. 21. Copyright © 1966 by the American Psychological Association. Reprinted by permission.

The memory function involves placing information into the memory store and must be distinguished from the memory store itself. The memory store underlies all the operations; all the abilities depend upon it. This is the most logical basis for supporting the idea that abilities increase with experience, depending upon the kinds of experience. The evaluative operation is concerned with assessment of information, cognized or produced, determining its goodness with respect to adopted criteria such as identity and consistency.

Guilford added the category of behavioral information on the basis of Thorndike's theory that there is a "social intelligence," distinct from what he named "concrete" and "abstract" intelligence. He decided to categorize "social intelligence" by kind of information, the kind that one person obtains from observation of another's behavior. Subsequent research by Guilford demonstrated a full set of six behavioral-cognition abilities as illustrated by the model, and a current analytical investigation is designed to test the part of the model that includes six behavioral systems, three parts of a four-part cartoon are given in each item, with four alternative parts that are possible completions.

There are four kinds of products: units, classes, relations, and systems, with illustrations. The other two kinds of products are transformations and implications. Transformations include any kind of change, movement in space, rearrangement or regrouping of letters in words or factoring or simplifying an equation, or rearranging events in a story.

Implied information is suggested by other information. Foresight or prediction depends upon extrapolating from given information to some anticipated future condition or event: "If I make this play in bridge, my side will be vulnerable."

The most immediate and important consequence of the theory and its model to Guilford and others has been its heuristic value in suggesting where to seek still undiscovered abilities.

Piaget's Theory of Intelligence

Many theorists define a series of stages in cognitive growth. Usually, these theories indicate that one stage grows out of the next and that the stages follow a certain invariable sequence. Most, but not all, of the theories include the assumption that each succeeding stage expands on and replaces the prior one, though there can be *vestiges* of the previous stage.

A major theorist in this regard is Jean Piaget, a Swiss psychologist, whose comprehensive observations of his own three children provided the basis for an entire elaborated and complex developmental theory, with cognitive development at its base. The significance of Piaget's work in Switzerland is often compared by some to Freud's contribution. Almost without help, over a span of fifty years, Piaget developed a comprehensive theory of cognitive growth and intelligence. Although his work shares many ideas with the learning theory, the Russian theory of intelligence, and ego psychology, it remains a unique and unequalled study of the function and development of the human mind.

For many years in the United States the scientific spirit of the time was such that the works of Piaget were buried in libraries, with many of his books not even translated into English. A renewed interest in cognitive development sparked a rediscovery of Piaget and a series of controlled experiments with children have verified many of the generalizations he made from his own observations. Subsequently, the theories and research stimulated by Piaget's work are regarded more and more as basically relevant to an understanding of the relationship between higher thought processes and social development.

During the entire developmental period, according to Piaget, the child is involved in building "schemata," which are organizations of relevant behaviors. Thus, there can be a "schema of sucking," which would include all the activities related to sucking: apprehension of the object to be sucked, activities of the mouth, lips, and hands during sucking, etc. The child's reactions or responses to the world are made up of schemata, but not exclusively; Piaget emphasizes schemata more in the earlier, simpler cognitive periods than in the later periods.

The acquisition of schemata occurs through a dual process of assimilation and accommodation. The first refers to the introjection of knowledge about the environment. This knowledge is then incorporated into the child's existing body of knowledge. In this incorporation process, the existing body is modified to accommodate the new elements. It is by this continuing dual process that schemata are organized and changed, that concepts are built and expanded.

Stages of Cognitive Development

Piaget assumed a series of stages in cognitive development, beginning with what he named the sensorimotor, progressing through the preoperational thought period to the period of formal operations. Age equivalents for these cognitive levels are not specific, with a fairly wide range of individual differences. A characteristic of the progression of levels is that the child becomes less dependent on particular external stimulation and better able to function in terms of symbols without concrete referents.

In the first period, the sensorimotor stages (0-2 years of age), the infant begins as a reflexive organism that responds to its environment in an undistinguishable manner. Later in this stage he becomes an organism that displays, as Flavell put it, "a relatively coherent organization of sensory-motor actions vis-a-vis his immediate environment." By the end of this stage, the infant has learned to distinguish external from internal stimuli by separating self from the external world. Objects remain the same when they are viewed from different angles. Learning takes place through the senses in conjunction with manipulation of objects.

The next stage, the preoperational (2-7 years of age) thought period, is preparation for the subsequent stage of concrete operations. This stage is subdivided into the preoperational phase (2-4 years of age) and the intuitive phase (4-7 years of age). In the preoperational phase, the child classifies by a single feature. For example, the child may classify an object either by color, shape or size (centering) but not by a combination of these. In the intuitive stage (not completely understood) there is a gradual awareness of conservation (Piaget uses conservation to mean that objects remain constant regardless of changes in their physical appearance). This stage is characterized by egocentricity and an irreversibility. Egocentricity means the child is unable to take another's point of view. He uses his own language. He cannot understand those who do not agree. Irreversibility describes the child's inability to return a concept to its point of origin. For example, addition is the opposite of subtraction.

By the end of the preoperational stage, the child is able to think in terms of classes, to see relationships, and to handle number concepts. He remains egocentric in his thought and relates everything to himself. Although his judgments are subjective, the basis has been laid for the development of logical operations.

The concrete operations stage (7-11 years of age) includes the growing ability to handle numbers, the development of a real logic, and the ability to relate external events to each other, independent of the self. The child can now classify and conceptualize the same person or object in more than one dimension. This period from 7 to 11 years of age is one of intense intellectual and conceptual development. At this point the child has the ability to think out problems that he previously worked out. He has also developed the ability to organize objects into a series and reverse operations (reversibility). During this period the student can understand that addition and subtraction are opposites. He can now decenter an object by looking at a combination of physical characteristics such as shape, size, and color. During the concrete operation stage the child begins to cooperate with others and develops an interest in games with rules. The rules of others are accepted guidelines to behavior where previously rules were formed as the game was played. Furthermore, the child can conceptualize the rules of other players.

The final developmental stage that Piaget defined is the period of formal operations (11 years of age and up). This is when the child develops true abstract thought and is able to develop hypotheses and logically test them. He has achieved conceptual independence from the concrete and can operate completely with symbols, with no need to introduce the concrete objects they represent. Adolescents begin to construct their own ideals and value systems and to evaluate hypotheses about their expanding world. At this point in time they begin to play for the future. They also have the ability to deal with contrary to fact propositions.

Within these stages are many substages and the development of conceptual frames, such as concepts of time and size. Included in Piaget's system are accounts of the development of perceptual, linguistic, mathematical, and moral concepts. It is a developmental and interactive system in the sense that development is seen to occur as a function of the contact between the child and his environment. None of these functions is presupposed to progress as described without environmental contact and interaction. The basic processes by which the development proceeds are accommodation and assimilation. Piagets maintains that intelligence is rooted in two biological attributes; adaptation and organization. Organization is the tendency for every living organism to integrate processes to coherent systems. For instance, an integration of the schemata of reaching and grasping. Adaptation is the innate tendency of a child to interact with his environment. This interaction fosters the development of a progressively complex mental organization. The preceding stage is understood to be the foundation of the subsequent stage. Adaptation is subdivided into accommodation and assimilation. The child assimilates information or experiences and builds an ever expanding structure of intelligence. Each new assimilation causes a new reaction with the environment and in turn, a more complex assimilation. When new experiences do not fit the child's existing intellectual frame work, accommodation occurs. This means the individual reacts in a modified manner.

Piaget's theory is one of knowledge, not of behavior. Learning is understood as being dependent on development. Learning varies with the child's available cognitive operations. The developmental stage determines what is learned and how it occurs. This has tremendous implications for the school curriculum. Marie Montessori's methods are the best known in this area and her techniques make use of children's spontaneous interests; she encourages children to work with materials as their wishes direct. Other researchers are developing curricula designed to foster the acquisition of the cognitive structures (Stendler-Lavatelli, 1968; Sigel, 1969; and Covington, 1970).

The question then arises: Is it possible to design educational experiences to increase the intellectual level of individuals? Yes, there seems to be evidence to this effect. It is generally accepted in psychological circles that the individual inherits a potential range of intelligence and the intellectual level actually developed is determined by environmental experiences. Human behavioral geneticists have concluded that approximately 80% of the variability in intelligence is caused by genetic structure and 20% by environmental influences (Cattell, 1965). Opportunities seem almost unlimited for the classroom teacher to provide enriching materials to stimulate the students.

The following is a summary outline of Piaget's stages of intellectual development:

I. Sensorimotor (Birth-2 years of age)
II. Preoperational (2-7 years of age)
   (a) Preoperational phase (2-4 years of age)
   (b) Intuitive phase (4-7 years of age)
III. Concrete Operations (7-11 years of age)
IV. Formal Operations (11 years of age and up)

Piaget based his complex theory of development on the rationale of equilibrium. The human is conceptualized as being in a constant state of disequilibrium or imbalance. Equilibrium is the unachievable ideal or utopia which humanity never reaches. The fact that one nearly accomplishes equilibrium creates disequilibrium. For example, the more one interacts with the environment, the more he is intellectually modified by the environment (sees things differently) because the individual has a new understanding of his environment. As a result of this interaction, the persons responses must change. This in effect is disequilibrium. Advertisement agencies use this concept to sell their wares. For instance, car sales indicate American consumers are never satisfied with last years model.

Intelligence Testing

As noted earlier in this chapter, intelligence involves an understanding of the relevant issues in new tasks and thinking of successful or satisfactory solutions to the tasks. The emphasis on novelty of the tasks serves the purpose of differentiating acts of intelligence from simple memory recall, although it is realized that memory has a role in reasoning. In intelligence tests, reasoning is emphasized, not concrete performances, because manual performances are easily influenced by a passing emotional stress and by training. Moreover, it is helpful to possess a measure of potential intelligence in order to have an estimate of what kind of work the individual could be doing. This potential power cannot be measured directly, but inferences may be drawn from the results.

Some factors should be kept constant in testing. Since test results depend, at least partially, on training (including any kind of pertinent experiences), interest, and effort as well as on intellectual capacity, it is important that training, interest, and effort be kept steadfast so that differences in intelligence can be measured in terms of differences in test scores. This requirement is met by (1) constructing tests measuring a wide range of mental tasks, (2) limiting the application of test norms to subjects who had at least the same educational opportunity as the norm population, and (3) assuring that the subject was sufficiently motivated in answering the test questions.

The reason for intelligence testing is to make educational or occupational plans for the future. Nontest estimates of intellectual capacity can be difficult, especially if the student's education has been irregular. The intellectual level is one of the most enduring and more important human traits.

Individuals with adequate intelligence may not achieve their potential for a variety of reasons, but no matter how hard a person with insufficient intelligence tries, he cannot achieve beyond his capacity. Frequently claims are made and alleged proofs are offered that intellectual capacity (the I.Q.) can be raised by proper training. But analysis shows that the improvement in the I.Q. on reexamination is spurious because motivation and cooperation differs from examination to examination.

Individual Tests. The Binet test is an individual test as are the others to be discussed in this section—the Terman version of the Binet test, the WAIS and the WISC. These tests are administered to one person at a time. In the Binet test, the intelligence quotient (I.Q.) is the ratio of mental age (MA) over chronological age (CA) multiplied by 100 to eliminate the decimal point. When chronological and mental ages are equal, the I.Q. is 100, that is, average. If the mental age is more than the chronological age, the I.Q. will be greater than 100, and if the chronological age is more than the mental age the I.Q. will be less than 100. An example might be the ten-year-old child who passes enough test items to get a mental age of 7. Then $\frac{MA7}{CA10} = 7 \times 100 = 70$. On the other hand, the ten year old who has a mental age of thirteen $\left(\frac{MA13}{CA10} = 1.3 \times 100 = 130\right)$ has an I.Q. of 130. Distribution of intelligence quotients in a normal population are represented in the following table.

Distribution of Intelligence Quotients in a Normal Population

Classification	IQ	Percentage Included
Very superior	140-170	1.5
Superior	120-139	11
High average	110-119	18
Average	90-109	46.5
Low average	80-89	14.5
Borderline	70-79	5.6
Mental defective	30-69	2.6

Taken from Terman and Merrill, 1960.

Another way of expressing the relative standing of an individual within his group is by percentile. The higher the percentile, the higher his rank within a group. For example, if an individual is at the 80th percentile level, he exceeds 80% of the group in the characteristic measured and is exceeded by only the remaining 20%. An I.Q. of 100 corresponds to the 50th percentile in intellectual ability for the general population. The intellectually lowest percentages are usually considered as mentally defective.

Terman's revision of the Binet test was succeeded by two newly revised and greatly enlarged comparable batteries L and M, of the 1916 tests published by Terman and Merrill in 1937. The new revisions ranged from the mental age of two years to the highest adult intellectual level. These tests have been largely displaced in clinical practice, however, by the Wechsler Adult Intelligence Scale (WAIS), published in 1939 and revised in 1955, and the Wechsler Intelligence Scale for Children (WISC), published in 1949. This displacement came about because of the difference in the content of many of the tests. The WAIS consists of tests of interest to adults. The Binet is designed primarily for children. However, the chief reason for preferring the WAIS and the WISC over the Terman tests is that considerable time is saved in administering the WAIS and the WISC. Unfortunately, this saving is made at some cost in accuracy. Both the WAIS and WISC are less discriminating in the youngest and oldest subject groups, and even among extreme of intellectual levels, than the 1937 Terman tests. The Terman tests are more accurate as measures of mental deficiency.

The Wechsler Adult Intelligence Scale (WAIS) is an intelligence test for adults and adolescents of both sexes from the age of 16 up. The scale is designed for individual administration and consists of six verbal and five nonverbal tests. Norms are provided for each of the tests, for the verbal test group, for the nonverbal test group, and for the entire scale. The order in which these single tests are given is not important.

David Wechsler, the originator of WAIS, suggested that the I.Q. computed on the entire scale be used as an indication of intellectual capacity. It may be desirable to use only the verbal test performance score in the calculation of the I.Q. because performance on the verbal tests is much less variable than that on the nonverbal tests. Also the verbal tests tend to resist the effects of emotional tension, psychosis, and brain disease more effectively than do nonverbal tests, unless there is damage to the speech areas.

A subject's I.Q. score indicates the degree of deviation of his intellectual capacity from the average. In this lies its importance. By general consensus, an I.Q. of 100 has been selected to denote average intellectual capacity on all intelligence scales. On the WAIS, the middle 50% of the adult and adolescent population (there are no sex differences) obtain I.Q.'s between 90 and 110. The lowest quarter obtain I.Q.'s below 90, and the lowest 5% obtain I.Q.'s of 75 or less. Analogously, the upper quarter obtain I.Q.'s over 110, and the highest 5% obtain I.Q.'s of 125 and over.

Group tests. Individual tests have the advantage of giving the examiner an opportunity to control cooperation and selected behavior patterns. This type of testing is time-consuming and requires skill and training. Some circumstances demand a test which can be administered quickly to a large group. Schools and the armed services are the most frequent users of group tests.

During World War I, there was a need to classify and categorize military recruits and to assign them expeditiously to duties appropriate to their abilities. It was also essential to determine quickly those recruits who could quickly learn to perform complex duties. This need gave rise to the development of group intelligence tests. A committee of distinguished psychologists used an unpublished test by Authur Otis to create the now famous Army Alpha group intelligence test, which with its many revisions has probably been administered to many millions. At the same time the Army Beta, a performance test, was devised to measure the intelligence of recruits who could not read or who spoke and read a language other than English.

These paper and pencil tests nearly always require good reading comprehension and are consequently unreliable with poor readers. They are speed rather than power tests and rely on questions where the answer is usually multiple choice. They are economical and convenient but much less reliable and valid than individual tests. It is not advisable to attempt predictions in the case of emotional disturbance because temporary emotional upsets interfere with speed of reading, responding, and understanding printed questions. Motivation during mass testing lags in many individuals. It is preferable to give an abbreviated individual test rather than a group test to the mentally disturbed. There are culture-free tests including the Army Beta Test and the Davis Eells Test of General Intelligence. Some tests of I.Q. have been charged with cultural bias. Under such a charge, the test results may be questionable.

The great advantage of standardized tests is that they are relatively precise in the assessment and provide standard norms against which a student's performance can be measured. The dependability of a test is always limited by its degree of validity and reliability. A test is valid if it actually serves the purpose for which it was intended. A test is reliable when it performs consistently. Test results are useful but limited in their applications.

The following are uses and limitations of group and individual test results.

Uses include:
a. Counseling—vocational, educational
b. Admission—Schools, Graduate, Medical, Dental, etc.
c. Placement—programs, jobs, courses

Limitations include:

(Both) a. Scores are not absolute, influenced by variables (estimate only)
(Group) b. Results are likely to change with age and experience
(Both) c. Tests are not error free
(Both) d. Lack of interpersonal relationship between child and examiner may exist
(Both) e. Child's over concern or lack of concern for the test
(Individual) f. Examiner skill and ability in administrating test, following directions and interpretation of the child's answers may be a problem
(Individual) g. Child's experiences prior to exam may effect the result
(Group) h. Directions are frequently misunderstood
(Group) i. Answers may be incorrectly placed on answer sheet
(Group) j. Excess test anxiety may occur
(Group) k. Poor reader or slow reader may be unable to complete the test
(Individual) l. Very expensive to use

Achievement tests published by a major publishing house are devised in essentially the same manner as those in the classroom. First, the terminal behavior is specified. Next the questions are written. They are then arranged in a trial form and administered to a representative sample. Items that appear to be more valid in terms of how well they discriminate between high and low scoring students are included in the test. The tests are then administered under controlled conditions and norms are established. Utilization of standardized tests by the classroom teacher involves administration and interpretation of scores.

Although a self-made examination may be interpreted in regard to thirty or more students, the interpretation of scores based on a nationwide sampling and administration is quite a different matter. Consequently, information is usually provided to make it possible to interpret a given student's raw score by norms relative to a class, school, district, state, or the entire nation. Usually achievement test scores are reported on profiles developed by the test publisher. The grade-equivalent score is established by interpreting raw scores in regard to grade level. For example, a student who made a grade-equivalent score of 4.8 performed at the level, the average fourth grader achieved by the eighth month. Caution should be exercised in interpreting a score that is above a student's actual grade level. This is not an indication that he is capable of consistently working at this level.

The universal score for achievement tests is the percentile rank. This score indicates the percentages of students who are at or below a particular student's score. Although it provides specific information about relative position, it has the disadvantage of deceptively revealing inaccurate relationships for students clustered around the middle of the distribution.

The standard deviation indicates the student's degree of deviation from the mean. This unit is of greatest value to the test interpreter when it is related to the normal probability curve. The normal probability curve is a mathematical concept that displays a hypothetical distribution of scores. Although such a distribution may rarely occur, it serves as a point of reference as to what would appear to be "normal" or "average." The standard deviation reveals how far a raw score lies from the mean of the distribution.

Stanines or standard nine-point scale scores were developed during World War II by Air Force psychologists. It is often used by test score publishers. This score divides the population into nine groups. With the exception of stanine 1 (the lowest) and stanine 9 (the highest), these groups are spaced in units of half a standard deviation.

Relationships of various scores may be conceptualized by viewing Figure 4.

Criterion-referenced Tests

There have been indications revealed in various educational periodicals recently that many educators in school districts and states are becoming interested in a type of testing that is basically different from the achievement tests that have been discussed in this text. Generally, these tests have been called criterion-referenced tests or objective referenced tests. These tests involve large numbers of specific instructional objectives from which an even larger number of test items have been derived. For instance, School Curriculum Objective Referenced Evaluation or SCORE, P.O. Box 30, Iowa City, Iowa 52240, offers more than 8,000 different objectives for grades K through 8 in the areas of reading, language arts, social studies, and mathematics. The Instructional Objectives Exchange or IOX, Dept. I, Box 24095, Los Angeles, California 90024, has a bank of cognitive and affective instructional objectives in more than fifty areas, such as study skills, decoding skills of reading, etc. The Evaluation of Individualized Instruction EII, 1400 West Maple Avenue, Downers Grove, Illinois 60515, project produced more than 4,500 objectives and 27,000 test items, including 645 objectives and 1,664 test items in the affective domain.

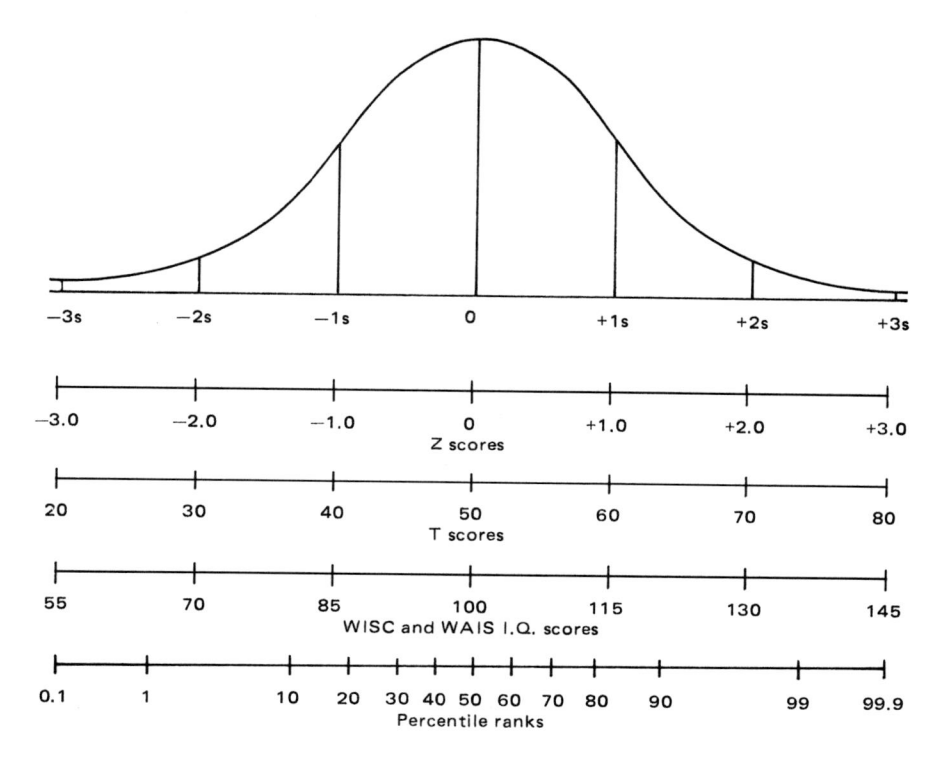

Figure 4. Relationship between T scores, z scores, WISC and WAIS Scores, and Percentile Ranks. Reprinted from *Psychology Applied to Teaching,* 2nd Edition by Robert Biehler. Copyright © 1974 by Houghton Mifflin Company. Used by permission.

SUMMARY

The teacher's understanding of cognitive development and intelligence is essential for effective student evaluation. Piaget's cognitive theory was discussed. Intellectual assessment was explored as viewed by Simon and Binet, Spearman, Thurstone and Guilford. Chapter 8 deals with the construction of student-centered behavioral objectives. Behavioral objectives are necessary in order to evaluate instruction and to communicate effectively the goals of the teacher.

STUDENT EVALUATION
STUDENT OBJECTIVES

In an objective type test which may include matching, multiple choice, and one word answers (fill in), the student will be able to:

(E)   1. Critically review a research article on intelligence and explain it to the class. (Written)
(K)   2. Define the following terms: (a) Intelligence, (b) Convergent, (c) Divergent, (d) Schema, (e) Assimilation, (f) Accommodation, (g) Validity, (h) Reliability, (i) Grade Equivalent, (j) Verbal and Performance Scores, (k) Basal and Ceiling Age, (l) Derivation I.Q.
(K)   3. Match the names of theorists with his/her theory of intelligence.
(C)   4. Explain the four major theories of intelligence discussed in class.
(An) 5. Discriminate between the major theories of intelligence discussed in class.
(K)   6. List the advantages of both group and individual I.Q. tests.
(K)   7. List three limitations of individual tests.
(K)   8. List three limitations of group tests.
(E)   9. Evaluate situations in order to determine which type of test to use, group or individual.
(C) 10. State and explain three uses of test results.
(An) 11. Discriminate between intelligence and achievement tests.
(E) 12. Interpret achievement test scores using the following systems: (a) Grade Equivalent, (b) Percentile, (c) Stanine.
(An) 13. Distinguish between norm and criterion referenced achievement tests.
(C) 14. Correctly interpret the following abbreviation: (a) SCORE, (b) IOX, (c) EII.
(K) 15. Match the correct address with the following banks for objectives: (a) School Curriculum Objective Referenced Evaluation, (b) Instructional Objective Exchange, (c) Institute for Educational Exchange.
(K) 16. Identify components of the major intelligence theories.
(C) 17. Give an example of each test: (a) I.Q. (Group and Individual), (b) Achievement.
(An) 18. Diagram or outline three of the four major intelligence theories.

Chapter 8

BEHAVIORAL OBJECTIVES

Behavioral objectives are usually defined as statements of purpose which describe student behavior and indicate the manner in which this behavior is to be exhibited. These statements describe what students will be able to do after completing a prescribed unit of instruction. For instance, a behavioral objective for a unit in history could be: "The student will be able to list five major factors which gave rise to World War II." Behavioral objectives serve two purposes. First, they are used by teachers to design, implement, and evaluate their instruction. Second, they are used to communicate the goals of instructional units to instructors who teach preceding and subsequent units and curriculum planners. Ammons (1964) surveyed 300 school systems and found that there were no objectives that described instructional goals in behavioral terms. When behavior was described they were of teacher behavior or vague and ambiguous in nature. They were not clearly defined. The need for the use of behavioral objectives within the classroom has been clearly documented.

HISTORICAL PERSPECTIVE

The earliest use of behavioral objectives in education and educational psychology occurred with Bobbitt (1918) and Charters (1923) when they expressed objectives in this fashion. Eugene R. Smith and others (1942) were among the earliest to use the term in outright expression of behavioral objectives. Taba (1962), Beauchamp (1961), Goodlad and Richter (1966), Hawthorne (1967), McClure (1965), Sand (1955), Krathwohl (1965), and Block (1965) are among those who have used the notion or idea of behavioral objectives in educational research and in curriculum development. McNeil (1966) makes a case for using behavioral objectives on the basis of supervision. He argues that when teachers and supervisors agree on what is to be accomplished evaluation becomes relatively easy in terms of identifying precisely what has been accomplished.

Mager (1962) makes an explicit description of behavioral objectives and focuses on two major qualifications not previously identified or discussed in the literature. These qualifications as he states them are that behavior must be observable and that the behaviors are terminal. On the other hand, Ammons (1967) argues for consideration of behavior which is

Behavioral objectives should be determined by empirical evidence.

not observable but which can be inferred according to definitions agreed upon by those involved in the learning process.

There are curriculum specialists who question the desirability of behavioral objectives. Among these are Eisner (1967) and Macdonald (1965). They argue that forming objectives prior to instruction may not be possible because the actual objective may change or emerge from the learning process.

In the widest application, the behavioral sciences represent the point of intersection of psychology, sociology, and anthropology, as well as many branches of education, economics, political science, and psychiatry. Historically, these disciplines have come into focus recently and have become an important aspect of contemporary culture. Many educators with an awareness of these disciplines attempt to integrate the understanding of behavior into their classroom discussions of literature, civics, current events, biology, history, and geography. Coupled with the recent demand for educational relevance and accountability, behavioral objectives offer a clear-cut method of making educational activities very precise and readily intelligible.

Interest in the education curriculum by behavioral scientists can be traced to William James. James wrote that it is important to impart a sympathetic conception of the mental life of pupils. He was invited and accepted Harvard's invitation to give public lectures to teachers on the subject. He proposed that the teacher make the student, not the subject, the focus of attention (James, 1899).

The behavioral sciences have not grown to the point where authoritative curriculum development is easily and quickly attainable; however, this does not mean that much has not been accomplished toward this goal. For instance, the National Science Foundation has supported interdisciplinary curriculum-oriented conferences. The American Psychological Association recently renamed its long standing Committee on High School Psychology the Committee on Precollege Psychology. This committee has planned a project to provide guidelines for the teaching of high school psychology and the training of teachers; it also plans to establish a newsletter and clearinghouse of information on precollege psychology. Independent organizations also have been attempting to integrate concepts in the behavior sciences and evolve relevant teaching units. For example, the Social Science Education Consortium, Inc., of Indiana has done several studies applicable to new social curriculum (Morrissett, 1967). The Education Department Center of Massachusetts has produced a social studies program entitled "Man: A Course of Study" (Bruner, 1965). It seems quite probable that the behavioral and social sciences will emerge in a more prominant role soon. Coupled with the fact that education "dollars" are more difficult to come by, administrators are ever more cognizant that instruction must count.

The idea for a classification system for behavioral objectives was structured at an informal meeting of college examiners attending the 1948 American Psychological Association Convention in Boston. It was at this meeting that a theoretical framework was pointed out as a need in the area of curriculum development. This conference felt that such a framework could do much to foster the exchange of test materials and ideas about testing. Additionally it could be helpful in stimulating research on the relations between testing and education. It was the conclusion of that meeting that such a theoretical framework could best be developed through a system of classification of the goals of the educational process, since educational objectives provide the basis for building curricula and tests and represent the starting point for much of educational research. This meeting was the first of a series of meetings of college examiners. Assembling at various universities each year and with some changes in membership, this group considered the problems involved in organizing a classification of educational objectives.

Some concern was expressed in the development of the classification system or taxonomy because some felt that such a scheme might cause educators to abort the thinking and planning process. Others expressed the fear that the taxonomy might lead to fragmentation of educational purposes. The original plans called for a complete taxonomy in three major parts—the cognitive, the affective, and the psychomotor domains. The cognitive domain includes those objectives which deal with the recall, recollection, or recognition of knowledge and the growth and development of intellectual abilities and skills. The affective domain includes objectives which describe changes in interest, attitudes, and values, and the development of appreciations and adequate adjustment. The third component is the manipulative or motor-skill area.

DEFINITIONS

Goals

It would be well to note here that the changes expected in student behavior may be considered either educational goals or educational objectives depending upon the level at which they exist. Goals, as stated earlier, usually represent the first step in translating the values and needs of society into the main stream of the educational program. Although they are deficient for making specific instructional assignments, they serve to present a panoramic picture of the total educational program and provide a perspective. The process of identifying and defining educational goals and objectives is a continual one. Educational goals reflect the philosophical statement of the institution and provide a point of origin or cornerstone for building reliable objectives. In most cases the desired end will be stated in very general terms, so general in fact that attempts to communicate specific intent may appear difficult.

Objectives

Objectives, as compared to goals, are relatively explicit formula of the ways in which student teachers are expected to change within education. Objectives may be viewed from the point of view of the teacher or student. These are referred to as either instructional objectives or behavioral objectives. An instructional objective is the behavior that a teacher is expected to perform in the teaching process. For example, the instructor will demonstrate the addition of like or unlike numbers. The behavioral objective describes the student's behavior after the teaching process has been completed. Three important characteristics of quality behavioral or instructional objectives are identified by curriculum experts as: (1) objectives must be visible; (2) there must be control over the conditions surrounding their attainment; and (3) there must be some commitment to their accomplishment. Objectives are operational definitions of goals. An effective operational step is to establish objectives on several different levels which may represent a hierarchy. The first level views the broad principle and philosophical statement involved. At the second level, one would establish operational objectives which assist in analyzing broad goals into refined components which are useful as building stones of a curriculum. Third, a level is needed which identifies specific learner behavior.

A typical objective might be that "the student will understand how to use the library." When a taxonomic structure is considered for objectives in terms of three large domains, specifically, the cognitive domain, the affective domain, and the psychomotor domain, the objective might be stated thusly: "When given the name of an author, the seventh-grade student will be able to list the holding in the library without the assistance of librarians or aides." Behavioral objectives should be written in such a way as to indicate what the learner will be able to do after an instructional event. This behavior will be directly applicable to a life situation or it may proceed to another instructional component.

Behavioral objectives may be either terminal objectives or enabling objectives. Terminal behavioral objectives are those which identify student action or performance on an entire unit. For example, a terminal objective for math might be: "At the conclusion of Math 101, the student will be able to satisfactorily derive the components for a truth table add fewer than four errors." Enabling objectives on the other hand are the component actions, knowledge, skills, etc., which a student must learn if he is to attain the terminal objectives. Enabling objectives represent the difference between where a student is now and where one wants him to be. Since terminal objectives are significant units, they become the means for organizing instruction. As such, they represent a performance level that is to be reached through instruction.

BLOOM'S TAXONOMY

A taxonomy is a useful tool in education because it provides comprehensiveness, communicability, stimulation in finding solutions to educational problems, and providing a basis for suggestions regarding methods in developing curricula, instructional techniques, and testing techniques. Such a classification scheme (taxonomy) can form the basis for instruments, techniques, and methods so that each teacher can determine the appropriateness of the work accomplished. Such a taxonomy aids in classifying student behavioral objectives, in construction of their objectives, and in detailed activities for lesson plans.

The following is an outline of the cognitive taxonomy as outlined by the *Taxonomy of Educational Objectives,* edited by Benjamin S. Bloom:

1:00 Knowledge: Those behaviors and test situations which emphasize remembering
- 1.10 Knowledge of Specifics: Recall of specific and isolable bits of information
- 1.11 Knowledge of Terminology: Knowledge of the referents for specific verbal and nonverbal symbols
- 1.12 Knowledge of Specific Facts: Knowledge of dates, events, persons, places, sources, etc.
- 1.20 Knowledge of Ways and Means of Dealing with Specifics: Knowledge of the ways of organizing, studying, judging, and criticizing
- 1.21 Knowledge of Conventions: Knowledge of characteristic ways of treating and presenting ideas and phenomena
- 1.22 Knowledge of Trends and Sequences: Knowledge of processes, directions, and movements of presenting ideas and phenomena
- 1.23 Knowledge of Classifications and Categories: Knowledge of the classes, sets, divisions, and arrangements which are regarded as fundamental for a given subject field, purpose, argument, or problem
- 1.24 Knowledge of Criteria: Knowledge of the criteria by which facts, principles, opinions, and conduct are tested or judged
- 1.25 Knowledge of Methodology: Knowledge of the methods of inquiry, techniques, and procedures employed in a particular subject field as well as those employed in investigating particular problems and phenomena
- 1.30 Knowledge of the Universals and Abstractions in a Field: Knowledge of the major schemes and patterns by which phenomena and ideas are organized
- 1.31 Knowledge of Principles and Generalizations: Knowledge of particular abstractions which summarize observations of pheomena
- 1.32 Knowledge of Theories and Structures: Knowledge of the body of principles and generalizations together with their interrelations which present a clear, rounded, and systematic view of a complex phenomenon, problem, or field

2:00 Comprehension: The lowest level of understanding

- 2.10 Translation: Comprehension as evidenced by the care and accuracy with which the communication is paraphrased or rendered from one language or form of communication to another
- 2.20 Interpretation: The explanation or summarization of a communication
- 2.30 Extrapolation: The extension of trends or tendencies beyond the given data to determine implications, consequences, corrollaries, effects, etc., which are in accordance with the conditions described in the original communication

3:00 Application: The use of abstractions in particular and concrete situations

4:00 Analysis: The breakdown of a communication into its constituent elements or parts such that the relative hierarchy of ideas is made clear and/or the relations between the ideas expressed are made explicit
- 4.10 Analysis of Elements: Identification of the elements included in a communication
- 4.20 Analysis of Relationships: The connections and interactions between elements and parts of a communication
- 4.30 Analysis of Organizational Principles: The organization, systematic arrangement, and structure which hold the communication together

5:00 Synthesis: The putting together of elements and parts so as to form a whole
- 5.10 Production of a Unique Communication: The development of a communication in which the writer or speaker attempts to convey ideas, feelings, and/or experiences to others
- 5.20 Production of a Plan, or Proposed Set of Operations: The development of a plan of work or the proposal of a plan of operations
- 5.30 Derivation of a Set of Abstract Relations: The development of a set of abstract relations either to classify or explain particular data or phenomena, or the deduction of propositions and relations from a set of basic propositions or symbolic representations

6:00 Evaluation: Judgments about the value of material and methods for given purposes
- 6.10 Judgments in Terms of Internal Evidence: Evaluation of the accuracy of a communication from such evidence as logical accuracy, consistency, and other internal criteria

6.20 Judgments in Terms of External Criteria: Evaluation of material with reference to selected or remembered criteria

The taxonomy defines a class or subclass of educational objectives from three points of view. The first definition is represented by a verbal description or definition of each class and subclass. The exact phrasing of this definition has been an issue. A second definition is stated in a list of educational objectives which are included under each subclass of the scheme. A third kind of definition attempts to clearly identify the behavior appropriate to each category by illustrations.

Objectives may be classified according to the level at which they are written. The guide for writing these objectives is *Bloom's Taxonomy*. For instance, objectives can be written from the knowledge (1.00) to the Evaluative level (6.00). At the knowledge level, "The student will be able to list advantages of . . ." requiring nothing more than rote memory. However, at the evaluative level, "The student will be able to constructively criticize. . . ." (Note: The higher levels of the system incorporate the lower levels. For example, a prerequisite for an objective written at the application level is information and processes from the knowledge and comprehension levels.)

CONSIDERATIONS

There are generally four major areas that are considered before educational goals and objectives are developed. These are: the educational purposes of the school or course; the learning experiences which can accomplish these goals; effective organizations of methods to help provide scope and sequence for the learner; and, how the effectiveness of the learning experiences can be evaluated by the use of tests or similar systematic data gathering procedures. Educational objectives are the explicit ways by which students are expected to be changed by the educational process. Final selection of objectives may rest on the training and past experiences of the teaching staff. It is highly probable that such a consideration of these four sources will result in a list of objectives which require more time and effort than is available. Consequently, the faculty must select those objectives that are feasible from objectives which are not likely to be achieved under the time and resources available.

CONSTRUCTION

The model used in this chapter in writing behavioral objectives is outlined in the CORD method, published in *CORD National Research Training Manual* (2nd ed.), edited by Jack Crawford of the Oregon State

System of Higher Education, with the contribution of ten authors. This document is available from ERIC under the number of ED 043136. The stated purpose of the manual is to present some principles useful in the systematic improvement of instruction. Nine chapters present a methodical approach to the design, implementation, and measurement of the effectiveness of an instructional system. The first four chapters are concerned with the development of an instruction system. The next three chapters outline methodological principles and techniques to measure the effectiveness of the instructional program while the last two deal with the administration of a research organization.

What are the parts of an objective? Writing behavioral objectives in appropriate form simply means stating a sentence where the subject, verb, and modifiers each have certain desired characteristics. The following mnemonics device may prove helpful in remembering how to write behavioral objectives. A behavioral objective may be divided into four component parts:

Audience: The subject of the behavioral objective sentence should describe who is doing the learning. It may simply be the grade level or class. For instance, "sixth-grade math students." Caution should be exercised at this point because all students will not achieve the same objectives within a given time. It is important that sufficient relevant descriptive information be included in the subject.

Behavior: The verb describes action, condition, a state of being of a behavioral objective. The verb should describe an observable action which the students will demonstrate. Some useful verbs are: identify, name, order, demonstrate, describe, construct, state a rule, apply a rule, interpret, and distinguish.

Conditions: Earlier it was stated that the purpose of behavioral objectives is not just to focus on what is observable, but also to render more observable that which is of interest. The success of this process will be determined by the care and ingenuity employed in describing the conditions of performance. It is here that one describes the setting for evaluation, the materials and aids the students will be given, and the nature of the problem that will be confronting them. A phrase describing the conditions might be: "Given a black outline map of the countries of Europe on which the international boundaries are indicated."

Degree: Rarely do all students master the behaviors described in the objective. If the degree of attainment is set too high it will cost too much in terms of educational resources. Realistic exceptations and the extent of mastery are essential considerations in stating degree.

The following points should be considered when writing instructional objectives:

1. Be certain of what you wish to accomplish with the population.
2. State operational objectives in a manner that will foster derivation of behavioral objectives.
3. Behaviors of intent must be observable and measurable.
4. Desired behaviors should be appropriate and consistent with the type of learning and specific content.
5. From the standpoint of design, the objectives should provide for a careful definition of the entry level of the audience for whom this specific instruction is intended.
6. Conditions under which these objectives are to be accomplished must be clearly defined.
7. The criterion selected must be related to the behavior in a relevant way. For instance, a time criterion is not relevant to a power objective such as "explain the lawmaking process of Tennessee."

In the writing process, one's concerns are directed to those kinds of behaviors to be accomplished immediately and those to be manifest in the future. It seldom happens that the behaviors described in an objective are completely mastered by all students in the population. Although these may be situations in which perfect mastery is required, the majority of instances more than likely will involve a compromise between the degree of attainment of the population and the expectations of the instructor. The degree of expectations and the degree of achievement must be approached realistically in writing behavioral objectives. Once an objective is established, the author of the objective has a commitment of insure that the students achieve it.

ADVANTAGES

The advantages of behavioral objectives are worth reiterating:

1. They provide efficiency in teaching.
2. They add efficiency in learning.
3. During an era of accountability, they provide an accurate evaluation of what has been accomplished by a student.
4. Because of public disenchantment with education today, demands are that instructors and administrators define very clearly and exactly what is to be accomplished academically.
5. Review of current teaching practices lend themselves to individualized instruction; consequently, some means and methods by which this can be accomplished is necessary. Behavioral objectives seem to fill the bill.
6. When behaviors are outlined clearly and with precision, it becomes a very simple matter to determine whether or not these have been met.

The family is a consideration in building educational goals.

SUMMARY

This chapter has dealt with the construction of student-centered behavioral objectives. The components of behavioral objectives were listed and defined. Finally, advantages of behavioral objectives for use by the classroom teacher were discussed.

In summary, this book has introduced the student of educational psychology to the major issues and current trends as they relate to the classroom teacher. An effort has been made not to restrict the student but to expand the boundaries of knowledge and to broaden the student's understanding of the individual's cognitive and personality development. The interaction of biological and environmental factors has been explored. The implications of the teacher's involvement in the human condition, and the possibilities for the enhancement of the quality of the life experience are awesome. This task is not to be taken lightly, but with a never ending search for new knowledge and answers.

CONSTRUCTING BEHAVIORAL OBJECTIVES
STUDENT OBJECTIVES

In an objective type test, which may include matching, multiple choice, and one word answers, the student will be able to:

- (K) 1. List the six levels of Blooms' Taxomony.
- (C) 2. Explain each of the six levels of Blooms' Taxonomy.
- (S) 3. Construct objectives at each level of Blooms' Taxonomy for a class or course of his or her choosing.
- (An) 4. Identify the level at which an objective is written.
- (K) 5. Define the following terms: (a) Goals, (b) Instructional Objectives, (c) Behavioral Objectives.
- (C) 6. Distinguish between each of the above terms, with examples.
- (S) 7. State the advantages and disadvantages to writing behavioral objectives.
- (C) 8. Paraphrase the CORD method of constructing behavioral objectives.
- (K) 9. List the 4 component parts of a behavioral objective as defined by the CORD method.
- (A) 10. Give examples of each component.
- (An) 11. Differentiate between the different components of behavioral objectives.
- (E) 12. Evaluate objectives written by fellow students using the CORD method.

REFERENCES

Akiskal, Hagop S., and McKinney, William T. (U Tennessee, Coll of Medicine) Overview of recent research in depression: Integration of ten conceptual models into a comprehensive clinical frame. *Archives of General Psychiatry,* 1975 (Mar), Vol 32(3), 285-305.

Ammons, Margaret. "An Empirical Study of Process and Product in Curriculum Development." *Journal of Educational Research* 57:451-57; 1964.

Ammons, Margaret. "Evaluation: What Is It? Who Does It? When Should It Be Done?" In *Evaluation of Children's Reading Achievement.* Perspectives in Reading Monograph Series. IRA, 1967.

Anderson, Dan W., and others. (Compilers.) *Strategies of Curriculum Development; Works of Virgil Herrick.* Merrill, 1965. 196p.

Asch, S.E. Effects of group pressure upon the modification and distortion of judgments. In H.S. Guetzkow (Ed), *Groups, Leadership, and Men.* New Brunswick, N.J.: Rutgers University Press, 1951.

Aspy, David N., and Buhler, June H. (Texas Women's U) The effect of teachers' inferred self-concept upon student achievement. *Journal of Educational Research,* 1975(Jul-Aug), Vol 68(10), 386-389.

Athanassiades, John C. (Georgia State U) An investigation of some communication patterns of female subordinates in hierarchical organizations. *Human Relations,* 1974(Mar), Vol 27(3), 195-209.

Bandura, Albert, and Walters, R. *Adolescent Agression,* Ronald, 1959, 475p.

Bandura, Albert. "Social Learning Through Imitation." In Marshall Jones (ed). *Nebraska Symposium on Motivation* University of Nebraska Press, 1962, pp. 211-269.

Bandura, Albert, and Walters, R. 1963.*Social Learning and Personality Development.* New York: Holt Rinehart and Winston.

Baron, Robert A., and Bell, Paul A. (Purdue U) Aggression and heat: Mediating effects of prior provocation and exposure to an aggressive model. *Journal of Personality and Social Psychology,* 1975(May), Vol 31(5), 825-832.

Barrett, Thomas C. "Taxonomy of Cognitive and Affective Dimensions of Reading Comprehension." University of Wisconsin, 1967. (Mimographed.)

Barton, George E., Jr. "Educational Objectives—Improvement of Curricular Theory About Their Determination." In Herrick, V.E., and Tyler, R.W. (Eds.) *Toward Improved Curriculum Theory.* University of Chicago Press, 1950, pp. 26-35.

Baughman, E. Earl. *Personality, The Psychological Study of the Individual,* Englewood Cliffs, N.J.: Prentice-Hall, 1972.

Beauchamp, George A. *Curriculum Theory.* Kagg, 1961. 149p.

Berenda, Ruth W. *The Influence of the Group on Judgements of Children.* New York: Columbia University Press, 1951.

Bestor, Arthur E. *Educational Wastelands: The Retreat from Learning in Our Public Schools.* University of Illinois Press, 1953. 226p.

Blair, G.L., Jones, R.S. and Simpson, R.H. *Educational Psychology.* Macmillan, 1975.

Block, Elaine C. "Sequence as a Factor in Classroom Instruction." Doctoral dissertation. University of Wisconsin, 1965.

Bloom, Benjamin S. (Ed.) *Taxonomy of Educational Objectives: Cognitive Domain.* Longmans, 1956. 207p.

Bobbitt, Franklin. *The Curriculum.* Houghton, 1918. 295p.

Bode, Boyd H. *Progressive Education at the Crossroads.* Newson, 1938. 128p.
Brubacher, John S. *Modern Philosophies of Education.* McGraw-Hill, 1939. 370p.
Bruner, Jerome. "The Growth of Mind." *American Psychologist,* Vol 20, 1965, p. 1013.
Bugental, James F.T. The Challenge That Is Man, *Challenges of Humanistic Psychology,* New York: McGraw-Hill Book Company, 1967.
Cattell, R.B. *The Scientific Analysis of Personality.* Baltimore: Penquin, 1965.
Charters, W.W. *Curriculum Construction.* Macmillan, 1923. 352p.
Covington, M.V. The Cognitive Curriculum: A Process-oriented Approach to Education. In J. Hellmuth (ed.) *Cognitive Studies,* Vol 1, New York: Brunner/Mazel, 1970, pp. 491-502.
Cox, Harvey. *Seduction of the Spirit,* Touchstone-Clarion, 1974.
Cox, Richard C. "An Overview of Studies Involving the Taxonomy of Educational Objectives: Cognitive Domain During Its First Decade." Paper presented at the meeting of the American Educational Research Association. Chicago, February 1966.
Crow, Lester D., and Crow, Alice. *Educational Psychology,* New York: American Book Company, 1963.
Dewey, John. *Theory of Valuation.* University of Chicago Press, 1939. 67p.
Eisner, Elliot W. "Educational Objectives: Help or Hinderance." *Sch. Rev.* 75:250-260; 1967.
Ekstrand, Gudrun. (Behavior in micro-drama situations and measures of creativity: An exploratory study.) (Swed) *Pedagogisk-Psykologiska Problem,* 1974 (Nov), No 258, 25p.
Falek, Arthur and Britton, Sharon. (Georgia Mental Health Inst. Human and Behavioral Genetics Research Lab, Atlanta) Phases in coping: The hypothesis and its implications. *Social Biology,* 1974(Spr), Vol 21(1), 1-7.
Finch, A.J.; Kendall, Philip C.; Montgomery, L.E., and Morris, Terry. (Virginia Treatment Ctr. for Children, Richmond) Effects of two types of failure on anxiety. *Journal of Abnormal Psychology,* 1975(Oct), Vol 84(5), 583-585.
Fleischer, Gerald. (Drexel U) Identification and imitation in the treatment of juvenile offenders. *Journal of Contemporary Psychotherapy,* 1975(Win), Vol 7(1), 41-49.
Garrison, Karl C. "A Study of Student Disciplinarian Practices in Two Georgia High Schools." *Journal of Educational Resources* 53 :153-156; 1959.
Goodlad, John I., and Richter, Maurice N., Jr. *The Development of a Conceptual System for Dealing with Problems of Curriculum and Instruction.* University of California at Los Angeles and Institute for Development of Educational Activities, 1966. 69p.
Goodlad, John I., and others. *The Changing School Curriculum.* Fund for the Advancement of Education, 1966. 122p.
Grant, David A. "Classical and Operant Conditioning" in Arthur W. Meton (ed.) *Categories of Human Learning.* Academic, 1964. pp.1-31.
Guszak. Frank J. "A Study of Teacher Solicitation and Student Response Interaction About Reading Content in Selected Second, Fourth and Sixth Grades." Doctoral dissertation. University of Wisconsin, 1966.
Hall, Calvin S., and Lindzey, Gardner. *Theories of Personality,* New York: John Wiley and Sons, Inc., 1970.
Harrison, Joseph E. "Achievement of Selected Types of Educational Objectives Through Use of Programmed Materials and the Relationship Between the

Achievement and Selected Aptitudes for Learning." Doctoral dissertation. University of Pittsburgh, 1964.

Havighurst, Robert J. *Developmental Tasks and Education*. University of Chicago, 1948. 86p.

Hawthorne, Richard D. "A Model for the Analysis of Team Teachers' Curricula Decisions and Verbal Instructional Interaction." Doctoral dissertation. University of Wisconsin, 1967.

Hebb, D.O. *A Textbook of Psychology*, ed. 2, W.B. Sanders, Philadelphia, 1966.

Henning, Carol J. "Discipline: Are School Practices Changing?" *Clearing House* 23:267-273; 1949.

Hewes, David D. On effective assertive behavior: A brief note. *Behavior Therapy*, 1975(Mar), Vol 6(2), 269-271.

Hicks, Leo. Apprentice Teaching and Exposure to Additional Information as Methods of Attitude Modification in Negro Schools, Ed.D. Thesis, Urbana, University of Illinois, 1967.

Hilgard, Ernest R., and Bower, Gordon H. *Theories of Learning*. 3rd. ed. Appleton, 1966. 661p.

Hull, Clark L. "Simple Qualitative Discrimination Learning" *Psychological Reports*. 57:303-313; 1950.

Humphrey, James H. (U Maryland) Teaching reading through creative movement. *Academic Therapy*, 1974(Spr), Vol 9(5), 321-323.

Husaini, Baqar A. (Tennessee State U) Achievement motivation and self-esteem: A cross-cultural study. *Indian Journal of Psychology*, 1974(Jun), Vol 49(2), 100-108.

James, William. Talks to Teachers on Psychology and to Students on Some of Life Ideals. New York: Holt and Co., 1899. p.50.

Jenkins, R.L., and Glickman, Sylvia. "Patterns of personality organization among delinquents" *Nervous Child* 6:329-339, 1947.

Jensen, Gale E. *The Validation of Aims for American Democratic Education*. Burgess, 1950. 124p.

Jensen, Larry C., and Rytting, Ann M. (Brigham Young U) Changing children's beliefs about punishment. *British Journal of Social and Clinical Psychology*, 1975(Feb), Vol 14(1), 91-92.

Kearney, Nolan C. *Elementary School Objectives*. Russell Sage, 1953. 189p.

Kilpatrick, William H., ed. *The Educational Frontier*. Century, 1933. 325p.

Kimble, Gregory A. *Hilgard and Marquis' Conditioning and Learning*. Appleton, 1961. 590p.

Klein, Frances. "Evaluation of Instruction: Measurement of Cognitive Behavior as Defined by the *Taxonomy of Educational Objectives*." Doctoral dissertation. University of California, Los Angeles, 1965.

Kohler, W. *The Mentality of Apes*. New York: Harcourt Brace Jovanovich, 1925.

Kohut, Heinz. (Reflections on narcissim and narcissistic anger.) *Psyche, Stuttgart*, 1973(Jun), Vol 27(6), 513-554. (German)

Korman, Abraham K. *The Psychology of Motivation* Englecliffs, N.J., Prentice-Hall, 1974, p.247.

Krathwohl, David R., and others. *Taxonomy of Educational Objectives: Affective Domain*. McKay, 1964. 196p.

Krathwohl, David R. "Stating Objectives Appropriately for Program, for Curriculum, and for Instructional Material Development." *Journal Teach. Ed.* 16:83-92; 1965.

Lindzey, Gardner, Hall, Calvin S., and Manosevitz, Martin (eds.) *Theories of Personality: Primary Sources and Research,* New York: John Wiley and Sons, Inc., 1973.
Loree, M. Ray. *Psychology of Education,* New York: The Ronald Press Company, 1970.
Macdonald, James B. "Myths About Instruction." *Educational Leadership* 22:571-576 + ; 1965.
Madsen, Charles H., Jr., and Madsen, Clifford K. *Teaching Discipline,* Boston: Allyn & Bacon, Inc., 1970, p. 43.
Mager, Robert F. *Preparing Instructional Objectives.* Fearon, 1962. 62p.
Martin, David G. *Personality: Effective and Ineffective,* Monterey, California: Brooks/Cole Publishing Company, 1976.
Maslow, Abraham. *Motivation and Personality.* Harper Row, 1954.
Maslow, Abraham. *Religion, Values and Peak Experiences.* Ohio State University Press, 1964. 123p.
Maslow, Abraham. Neurosis as a failure of personal growth, *Humanitas,* 1967, 3, 153-170.
Maslow, Abraham. *Toward a Psychology of Being.* Van Nostrand, Princeton, N.J., 1968.
McCarthy, Mary D. Humanitarianism and corporal punishment. *Education,* 1975(Spr), Vol 95(3),212-215
McClure, Robert M. "Procedures, Processes, and Products in Curriculum Development." Doctoral dissertation. University of California, Los Angeles, 1965
McNeil, Elton B. *The Psychology of Being Human,* San Francisco: Canfield Press, 1974.
McNeil, John D. "Antidote to a School Scandal." *Educational Forum,* 31:69-77; 1966
Meissner, W.W. The role of imitative social learning in identicatory processes. *Journal of the American Psychoanalytic Association,* 1974, Vol 22(3), 512-536.
Miller, Neal E. "Liberalization of Basic S-R Concepts: Extensions to Conflict, Behavior, Motivation, and Social Learning." In Koch, Sigmund (ed.) *Psychology: A Study of Science.* Vol 2, McGraw Hill, 1959. pp. 196-292.
Miller and Dollard, *Social Learning and Imitation,* Yalt Press, 1941.
Minuchin, P. Sex-role concepts and sex-typing in childhood as a function of school and home environments, *Child Development,* 1965, 36, 1033, 1033-1048.
Mischel, Harriet N. and Mischel, Walter. *Readings in Personality,* New York: Holt, Rinehart and Winston, Inc., 1973.
Morse, W.C. and Wingo, G.M. *Psychology and Teaching,* Scott, Foresman, 1969.
Morrissett, Irving. Aids in the Development of Soc Science Ed in the Midwest. Ed 010 086 (ERIC).
Osterhouse, Robert A. (U Maryland) Classroom anxiety and the examination performance of test-anxious students. *Journal of Educational Research,* 1975(Mar), Vol 68(7), 247-250.
Pavlov, Ivan P. *Conditional Reflexes,* Translated G.V. Aniep. Oxford University Press, 1927. 420p.
Redl, Fritz, and Wattenberg, W.W. *Mental Hygiene in Teaching,* Harcourt, 1959. 562p.
Redl, Fritz. *When We Deal with Children.* New York Free Press, 1966.

Replogle, Vernon Loyal. "The In-fold Approach to Elementary School Curriculum: An Examination of Major Curricular Approaches and a Proposal Based on Social Realities, Needs, and Values in Interaction." *Microfilm Abstracts* 11:941-942; 1951.

Ricks, Nancy L., and Mirsky, Allen F. (Boston U, Medical School) Sustained attention and the effects of distraction in underachieving second grade children. *Journal of Education,* Boston, 1974(Nov), Vol 156(4), 4-17.

Russell, George D. "The Development of a Classification of Educational Objectives to Study the Objectives of Four Community Adult Education Agencies. Doctoral Dissertation University of Wisconsin, 1964.

Sahakian, William S. (ed.) *Psychology of Personality: Readings in Theory,* Chicago: Rand McNally College Publishing Company, 1974.

Sand, Ole. *Curriculum Study in Basic Nursing Education.* Putnam, 1955. 225p.

Sanders, Norris M. *Classroom Questions: What Kinds?* Harper, 1966. 176p.

Sandmeier, Thelma L. "A Study of the Differences in Aims for Public Elementary Education as Related to Selected Sociological Factors." Doctoral dissertation. Rutgers State U, 1964.

Saylor, Galen. "Don't Just Do Something. *Educational Leadership.* 17:2-5; 1959.

Schaller, Joseph. (U Goteborg, Sweden) Experienced and expected problems reported by children after a family move. *Goteborg Psychological Reports,* 1974, Vol 4(16), 12p.

Schrupp, M.H. and Gjerde, G.M. "Teacher Growth Behavior Problems in Children." *Journal Educational Psychology* 44:203-14, 1953.

Sigel, J.E. The Piagetian system and the world of education. In D. Elkind and J.H. Flavell (eds.), Studies in Cognitive Development: Essays in Honor of Jean Piaget. London: Oxford University Press, 1969, pp. 465-489.

Skinner, B.F. *The Behavior of Organisms: An Experimental Analysis.* Appleton, 1938. 457p.

Skinner, B.F. *Science and Human Behavior.* Macmillian, 1953. 461p.

Slobetz, "Elementary Teachers' Reactions to School Situations." *Journal of Educational Research,* Vol 44, October 1950, pp. 81-90.

Smith, B. Othanel and others. *Fundamentals of Curriculum Development,* rev. Ed. World, 1957. 685p.

Smith, Eugene R., and others. *Appraising and Recording Student Progress.* Harper, 1942. 550p.

Smith, Henry Clay. *Personality Development,* New York: McGraw-Hill Book Company, 1968.

Snider, Sarah J., and Murphy, W. Carl. (Carson-Newman Coll) Discipline: What can it teach? *Elementary School Journal,* 1975(Feb), Vol 75(5), 299-303.

Spence, Kenneth W. "The Differential Response in Animals to Stimuli Varying Within a Single Dimension." *Psychological Reports* 44:430-444; 1937.

Steers, Richard M. (U Oregon Graduate School of Management and Business) Task-goal attributes, achievement, and supervisory performance. *Organizational Behavior and Human Performance,* 1975(Jun), Vol 13(3), 392-403.

Stendler-Lavatelli, C.B. Environmental intervention in infancy and childhood. In M. Deutsch, I. Katz, and A.R. Jensen (eds.) *Social Class, Race and Psychological Development.* New York: Holt, Rinehart, and Winston, 1968, pp. 347-380.

Stouffer, George A.W., Jr., and Owens, Jennie. "Behavior Problems of Children as Identified by Today's Teachers and Compared with Those Reported by E.K. Wickman." *Journal of Educational Resources* 48:321-331; 1955.

Taba, Hilda. *Curriculum Development; Theory and Practice.* Harcourt, 1962. 529p.

Teevan, Richard C., and Smith, Barry D. (State U New York, Albany) Relationships of fear-of-failure and need achievement motivation to a confirming-interval measure of aspirational levels. *Psychological Reports,* 1975(Jun), Vol 36A.(3), 967-976.

Terman, Lewis M., and Maud A Merrill. *Measuring Intelligence.* Boston: Houghton Mifflin, 1937.

Terman, Lewis M., and Maud A. Merrill. *Stanford-Binet Intelligence Scale,* Boston: Houghton Mifflin Co., 1960. 18p.

Thorndike, E.L. *Human Learning.* Appleton-Century-Crofts. New York, 1931.

Touliatos, John, and Lindlhom, Byron W. (Auburn U) TAT need achievement and need affiliation in minimally brain-injured and normal children and their parents. *Journal of Psychology,* 1975(Jan), Vol 89(1), 49-54.

Tyler, Ralph W. *Basic Principles of Curriculum and Instruction.* U Chicago, 1950. 83p.

Valentine, Jr., Lonnie D., and Vitola Bart M. Comparison of self motivated air force enlistees with draft motivated enlistees July, 1970. vii + 18 + (2) p. 4, Proj 7717 task 771705.

Vansina-Cobbaert, Marie-Jeanne. S. Freud's views on the relationship between incorporation, introjection and identification. *Psychologica Belgica,* 1974, Vol 14(2), 83-92.

Wickman, E. Koster. Children's Behavior and Teachers' Attitudes. The Commonwealth Fund, 1928. 247p.

Wiggins, Jerry, S., Renner, K. Edward, Clore, Gerald L., Rose, Richard J. *Principles of Personality.* Reading, Mass.: Addison-Wesley Publishing Company, 1976.

Windeknecht, Thomas G., and D'Angelo, Henry. (Memphis State U) The stereotype approach to the modeling and simulation of an elementary school. *IEEE Transactions on Systems, Man. and Cybernetics,* 1975(Mar), Vol 5(2), 216-225.

Woodworth, R.S. *Dynamic Psychology,* Columbia University Press, 1918. 50p.

Workman, Edward A., and Stillion, Judith M. (Western Carolina U) The relationship between creativity and ego development. *Journal of Psychology,* 1974(Nov), Vol 88(2), 191-195.